SHOOTING THE PAST

a screenplay

Stephen Poliakoff, born in 1952, was appoin
National Theatre for 1976 and the same year
Most Promising Playwright award for *Hitting*
also won a BAFTA award for the Best Single Play for *Caught on a Train* in
1980 and the *Evening Standard*'s Best British Film award for *Close My Eyes*
in 1992. His plays and films include *Clever Soldiers* (1974), *The Carnation
Gang* (1974), *Hitting Town* (1975), *City Sugar* (1975), *Heroes* (1975),
Strawberry Fields (1977), *Stronger than the Sun* (1977), *Shout Across the River*
(1978), *American Days* (1979), *The Summer Party* (1980), *Bloody Kids*
(1980), *Caught on a Train* (1980), *Favourite Nights* (1981), *Soft Targets*
(1982), *Runners* (1983), *Breaking the Silence* (1984), *Coming in to Land*
(1987), *Hidden City* (1988), *She's Been Away* (1989), *Playing with Trains*
(1989), *Close My Eyes* (1991), *Sienna Red* (1992), *Century* (1994), *Sweet
Panic* (1996), *Blinded by the Sun* (1996), *The Tribe* (1997) and *Talk of the
City* (1998).

10 9 8 7 6 5 4 3

Copyright © 1998 by Stephen Poliakoff
The right of Stephen Poliakoff to be identified as the author
of this work has been asserted by him in accordance with the
Copyright, Designs and Patents Act, 1988

Photocredits cover and inside: Talk Back, Joss Barratt, Liam Daniel,
Sven Arnstein, BBC

First published in Great Britain in 1998
by Methuen Publishing Limited

Methuen Drama
A & C Black Publishers Ltd
38 Soho Square, London W1D 3HB

A CIP catalogue record for this book is available from the British Library

ISBN 978-0-413-73140-1

Typeset by MATS, Southend-on-Sea, Essex
Printed and bound in Great Britain by
Cox & Wyman Ltd, Reading, Berkshire

SHOOTING THE PAST

Stephen Poliakoff

Methuen Film

Shooting the Past was produced by Talkback Productions Ltd for BBC Television and screened in November 1998 by BBC2. The cast was as follows:

Oswald	Timothy Spall
Marilyn	Lindsay Duncan
Anderson	Liam Cunningham
Spig	Emilia Fox
Nick	Blake Ritson
Veronica	Billie Whitelaw
Garnett	Arj Barker
Styeman	Andy Serkis

Producer John Chapman
Production Designer John-Paul Kelly
Directors of Photography Bruno de Keyser and Ernest Vincze
Director Stephen Poliakoff

SHOOTING THE PAST

Play One

EXT. NIGHT.

A series of Christmas shots, street decorations, shop windows, trees, starting in the West End and moving northwards.

The images dissolving into each other, gathering in pace all the time, leading us towards OSWALD's *face.*

From Knightsbridge, we move through Regent Street, then through a street in London where an ordinary council house is completely covered with coloured lights and glowing Father Christmases and on to OSWALD's *street with its series of turreted houses.*

A turret near his house has a dangle of Christmas lights on it.

INT. DAY. OSWALD'S ROOM.

OSWALD's *large moon-shaped face staring straight at us.*

It is difficult to tell exactly how old he is, he has a slightly dishevelled appearance, and he is sitting wrapped up in an old-fashioned cardigan. He could be in his forties or fifties.

He fixes us with his gaze, which one moment is deadly serious, a second later there is a flash of anarchic humour . . . but when he speaks, there is a compelling finality about his tone.

OSWALD: So – I have no idea if this is going to work. But it really is the best way I can think of doing it.

> *He eats something for a moment, we can't see what it is because he is staring at us in giant close-up. He chews, making rather a lot of noise. He continues.*

First of all, clearly I don't have a video camera . . . For the only time in my life it would have helped having one . . . (*Staring at us for a moment.*) . . . But it seemed a bit bloody late to buy one. (*He grins.*) This being the last afternoon of my life . . . (*He brushes crumbs from his lips.*) But because I want to leave a record of the extraordinary events that have happened these last few days . . . I'm talking into this.

3

We see OSWALD *is talking into a battered old Dictaphone dating back to the late sixties.*

Ridiculously out of date of course . . . and I haven't used it since I practised doing football, and cricket commentaries on it at the age of twelve and three-quarters.

But it does *work* . . . it's still functioning . . . rather good quality in fact.

And every now and then I will take a picture of myself. That's not strictly necessary I know . . . but I want to do that . . .

We see he is facing a stills camera, mounted across the room. He is operating the flash from where he is sitting.

Together they will form something hopefully that can be kept, published, even used by the mass media.(*He stops.*)

Not even – I shouldn't have said that – *must* be used by the mass media.

He takes another bite. We see he is eating melted cheese on toast with slices of tomato, from an enamel plate in front of him.

So why the hell should they be interested in a chubby man, wearing a cardy – talking into an old tape machine?

How could this be a blazingly urgent . . . ?

He watches the tape spool go round for a moment.

Vitally important . . .

He stops the tape, pulls himself up out of the chair and stares into the mirror, inspecting his moon-shaped face for a moment. We see the clutter in his room for the first time.

(*To himself.*) Come on, Waldy, you were doing really well . . .

He sits again staring at us, sitting slightly forward on the edge of his chair this time. He takes another bite of the toast. He smiles broadly.

Why should we care? Or rather why should *you* care?

Because what hit me with such a wallop – and it was a

wallop – could happen to anybody . . . Has happened to a lot of people. Anybody who suddenly loses their job, or their house even . . . or has somebody promoted above them . . . Anybody who knows how that feels – this is for you . . .

He munches.

He curls a piece of melted cheese away from the toast and eats it. Then he stares at us.

And there's the added spice – was it all my fault, was it *all* entirely caused by yours truly?! I don't think for a moment it was – I think that's absolute total bollocks . . . but it is only fair to mention – for the record – there are those who do think that.

He picks up toast.

Anybody that finds me and who rushes to judgement (*He grins.*), *beware.* So . . . when I've finished this piece let's get going . . .

He chews for a moment thoughtfully staring at a piece of tomato.

So it is December the twenty-first and we're in London . . .

He chews for a moment thoughtfully.

It's slightly amazing to think that was only a few days ago this started.

Takes out napkin. OSWALD *grins.*

I've made myself rather hungry eating that now – (*He glances around.*) OK, I'll wait . . .

So – a large eighteenth-century house, not far from central London.

EXT. LARGE EIGHTEENTH-CENTURY HOUSE. DAY.
Travelling shots round the exterior of the house and its gardens, and viewing it across the neighbouring park. We see it's nestling on the edge of London.

OSWALD (*voice-over*): This house was built for his mistress by the Earl of Halifax . . .

But when they had finished with it, it fell on hard times, until a great nineteenth-century confectionery firm rescued it. They were famous for their chocolates and toffees – apparently the greatest toffees of the age.

Like a lot of nineteenth-century firms they had philanthropic leanings – and they started an Institute for the Improvement of Londoners, in this house.
We see details of the fine decorations inside the house, including the gold leaf in the cafeteria and a Latin inscription on the wall 'whatever you do, do cautiously, and look to the end'.

INT. HALL. GROUND FLOOR.
The camera begins to move down a long curving passage.

OSWALD (*voice-over*): Somehow, nobody is quite sure how, they also began collecting photographs, and this flowered during the years into the Fallon photo library and collection – and it just grew and grew!
The camera goes round a corner and begins to move towards some double doors.
After the war the Institute passed into the hands of an insurance company, rather a benign outfit, who kept out of the way in one part of the house.
The camera continues moving towards the partially opened doors.
And the Fallon collection and photo library continued to be run as a quiet business, left to its own devices as all businesses should! Paying its way, or we thought it was.
And besides –
The camera is staring through the glass. On the other side of the doors we can just make out the shadowy lines of shelves

stretching away into the darkness.

And besides, it is an exceptionally magical place, as you will see . . .

INT. OSWALD'S ROOM. DAY.
We cut back to OSWALD's *room.* OSWALD *is staring straight at us.*

OSWALD: At last our friendly insurance company sells up and leaves London – and the day comes . . . we are to meet our new owners.

    We have no idea – nobody believes me! . . . But we have NO IDEA what kind of day it was to be. No inkling that it was to be such a momentous, mind-shattering, sort of day . . .

INT. GALLERY. DAY.
We see MARILYN *walking towards us. A woman in her late thirties or early forties. She is dressed in a smart but restrained way, in contrast to the shabby appearance of* OSWALD. *There is at first sight a formidable quality to* MARILYN – *the unmistakable feeling of a headmistress, or of any other individual that rules her own world. But she has an intense warm smile that breaks out, suggesting a more sensual, volatile side that suddenly appears underneath the rather strict demeanour.*

INT. GROUND HALL. DAY.
As MARILYN *walks towards us,* SPIG, *a young girl of about twenty, runs away from the camera towards* MARILYN *calling:*

SPIG: They're here! I've seen them, they're here already!

MARILYN: It's OK, there's no need to rush, they can wait a moment.

SPIG *rushes back into the entrance hall, stares out of a side window, we get a partially obscured view of the outside world.*

Everything about the interior of the building suggests a contained orderly world, untouched by the outside.

We see from SPIG*'s POV a large car, and a tall rather elegant man in his forties getting out of the back seat, he is accompanied by a colleague who keeps a respectful one step behind.*

MARILYN, OSWALD *and the other inhabitants of the building,* VERONICA, *a nervous twitchy woman in her late fifties, and* NICK, *a very tall quiet boy of nineteen, are all standing in a welcoming party.*

OSWALD *is sitting on the edge of a table in the hall, swinging his legs like a large oversized boy.*

SPIG *opens the door as* ANDERSON *and his colleague move towards us.*

MARILYN: Here we are . . . (*She smiles a warm welcoming smile.*) Ready for you . . . and you're splendidly punctual – which is a very good start. I'm Marilyn Truman.

ANDERSON: Christopher Anderson . . .

ANDERSON *is American and although he's dressed in a business suit and is accompanied by* GARNETT, *who looks like an accountant, there is something, too, of the academic about* ANDERSON, *a rather gentle almost refined manner.*

MARILYN: So this is Oswald . . . Oswald Bates, who if you like is second in command here – not that we use terms like that . . . and this is Veronica.

VERONICA *bobs a sharp bird-like greeting.*

MARILYN: And then the two young ones, Spig, who insists we call her that . . . and Nick (*She smiles at the quiet boy.*) – who never wants to be called anything.

Now come this way . . . I'm sure you want the grand tour.

OSWALD (*sitting swinging his legs*): We're going to give you the grand tour, whether you like it or not . . .

ANDERSON (*surprised by this*): The grand tour?

INT. GALLERY. DAY

MARILYN *is already leading the way, her manner is totally sunny though there is great authority about the way she moves through her domain.*

MARILYN (*as they move down the passage*): Fortunately the one thing we have is space . . . we do have lots of space.

GARNETT (*in a warning tone*): Mr Anderson does have a meeting on site in a few minutes.

The passage leading to the cafeteria has a couple of black and white photos displayed, rather teasingly, as a trailer for the main collection.

INT. CAFETERIA. DAY.

The cafeteria is a splendid room, the two dinner ladies preparing food in the background in a white tiled kitchen. And the table is formally laid out with a spread for the visitors of buns, sandwiches and drinks.

MARILYN: And somehow we still have our own in-house cooking – even though there are only five of us! (*She laughs.*) Rather wicked I know . . .

OSWALD *has moved behind the table spread with food.*

OSWALD: So we've laid on what we thought would appeal . . . doughnuts of course . . . Californian wine – maybe a little later! A full elevenses anyway – so you can make complete pigs of yourselves.

9

We can see ANDERSON *staring about him. We can sense something is wrong, that he is feeling a gathering sense of quiet anger.*

MARILYN: And if you're really starving, and none of this appeals (*Indicating dinner ladies.*), Molly might just rustle up something hot.

OSWALD (*glinty look*): Her roly-poly pudding is justly famous.

ANDERSON (*suddenly*): Ms Truman, I need to have a word.

MARILYN: Of course. Fire away.

ANDERSON: I need a *private* word.

INT. MARILYN'S OFFICE. DAY.
We cut to MARILYN's *office. A large room, but very sparingly decorated. The furniture is extremely elegant though, and the room is dominated by a rather magnificent antique desk.*

MARILYN *is standing by the desk, and she indicates graciously where* ANDERSON *should sit.*

ANDERSON *catches a glimpse of the collection through the other door of the room, which is slightly open. As he is peering,* SPIG *suddenly appears out of the shadows of the collection and closes the door from the other side.*

MARILYN's *manner is very breezy, she has clearly no idea what is coming.*

MARILYN: So do tell me exactly what you're doing with the rest of the building – it's becoming a Business School isn't it?

ANDERSON (*staring across at her*): Yes . . . (*He lifts his hand to still her flow.*)

MARILYN: A sort of American LSE? Is that right . . . ? (*Then translating.*) That is the London School of Economics . . . (*She is keeping an eagle eye on* GARNETT *who is fiddling with one of the ornaments on the mantelpiece.*) There are a lot of rather suspicious colleges dotted about this city, I gather, the American School of this and that. (*She smiles.*) But of course you won't be one of those – altogether a higher class of establishment, I'm sure.

ANDERSON (*having to raise his voice to stop her*): Ms Truman, please . . .

MARILYN *turns in surprise at his tone.*

ANDERSON: I don't think you realise.

MARILYN: Realise what?

ANDERSON: That there has been . . . (*He stops for a second.*) There seems to have been a major breakdown in communication.

MARILYN: Really? In what way? I don't believe so . . . Here you are – (*She smiles.*) and elevenses was waiting for you . . .

ANDERSON: I have no idea how this has happened – because you have acknowledged all our letters, and said you understood exactly.

GARNETT: *Every* letter we sent you was replied to.

MARILYN *turns startled.*

ANDERSON: You *must* know, Ms Truman?

MARILYN: No. (*Nervous laugh.*) We can do this all day – a guessing game . . . I have no idea what you're talking about.

ANDERSON: Do you want to sit?

MARILYN *very surprised to be asked to sit in her own office.*

MARILYN: No thank you. I'm quite happy like this.

ANDERSON: Ms Truman . . . The library . . . your business . . . is being closed.

Pause.

MARILYN: Closed? That's ridiculous! Who's closing it?

ANDERSON: It's not ridiculous. It is what is happening.

(*Turning to Garnett.*) We'll have copies of the

correspondence faxed to you . . . (*Back to* MARILYN.)
But I'm sure you must have seen them.

MARILYN (*suddenly flashing out of her*): What do you mean I
must have seen them? . . . You think I'm play acting?!
This is absolutely the first time I've heard this.

GARNETT: The letters were sent to Mr Bates. To a Mr
Oswald Bates.

MARILYN *is trying hard to remain calm.*

ANDERSON: And several months ago as well – the notice of
closure . . .

MARILYN: Well, 'closure' is impossible clearly. The
collection, the library is over a hundred years old. It is
out of the question – I don't know how you normally do
business . . . but coming in here, just walking in, and
saying you're shutting the place, it is inconceivable that
that can happen . . .

ANDERSON*'s mobile phone rings.*

ANDERSON (*into phone, his voice quiet, restrained*): Marty . . .
yes, I've not quite got there yet, as soon as I reach . . .
there . . . no I'll get a revised costing, no . . . no there's
no need for that, I'll be there in a few minutes. (*He
glances over in* MARILYN*'s direction*) Excuse me a
moment . . . (*Back into phone.*) No no, everything's fine –
the schedule's tight, but manageable.

MARILYN *suddenly moves out of the room.*

INT. GROUND FLOOR HALL. DAY.
We cut to the passage outside the office. SPIG, NICK *and*
VERONICA *are sitting in a nervous row in the passage, staring
at the door, fidgeting in the strong morning sunlight.*

OSWALD *is nonchalantly wandering up and down humming
to himself, a surreal medley of tunes, some from the* Sound of
Music, *and a snatch of Beethoven's Seventh Symphony.*

MARILYN *walks straight up to* OSWALD.

12

MARILYN: Do you know what they just told me?

OSWALD: What? Let me guess – they don't like the elevenses? They were offended by the doughnuts?

MARILYN (*lowering her voice*): Oswald – did you at any time receive a letter saying they were shutting us down?

OSWALD: Shutting us down?! Absolutely not.

MARILYN *is staring straight into his moon-shaped face.*

OSWALD: Not a single word.

MARILYN: Never?

OSWALD: Never. (*He stares at her.*) I promise.

MARILYN: And you didn't reply to any letters?

OSWALD: If I didn't receive any, how could I reply?

MARILYN (*quiet*): I thought so . . .

OSWALD: They can't shut us down.

MARILYN: I know.

OSWALD (*whispers very close*): Don't accept anything . . . don't accept one single thing – not even their right to be in our office . . .

INT. MARILYN'S OFFICE. DAY. (DOOR OPEN.)
We cut back inside MARILYN*'s office as* MARILYN *enters. She is presented with the sight of both men on their mobile phones.* ANDERSON *acknowledges her as he talks on the phone,* GARNETT *is in a corner of the room discussing figures. For a second,* MARILYN *watches them.*

MARILYN: I think since we happen to be in my office, maybe we can deal with this *first*.

ANDERSON (*into phone*): I told you I would be going straight over there. (*He smiles into phone.*) No it won't be as bad as that. No way. (*He rings off.*)

MARILYN: Well, I've talked to my staff – and there has been no correspondence, no correspondence with you, as I thought. No prior warning, not one hint . . .

GARNETT (*simply*): They are lying to you.

MARILYN *remains icy calm, she turns to* GARNETT.

MARILYN: I think you'd be extremely well advised not to make any more remarks like that.

ANDERSON: What Bill meant was it just cannot be the case. (*Staring at* MARILYN.) What you say cannot have happened. We have just checked, we know for a fact there were at least four letters sent to Mr Oswald Bates – (*Trying to conceal the amazement in his voice.*) We were advised Mr Bates dealt with all the *business* side of the library – and we received replies to all these letters saying that you were taking all necessary steps to comply.

MARILYN *is moving across the room,* ANDERSON *is sitting on the corner of her desk now, she instinctively doesn't want to concede any physical ground to him.* GARNETT *has opened the door to the collection, we see the shadowy aisles stretching into the distance.*

MARILYN: We were taking necessary steps, were we? (*She stares at both men.*) What did those letters say we were complying with exactly?

ANDERSON (*patiently*): They said these buildings were to be developed, and become the headquarters of the American School of Business for the Twenty-First Century – or the Twenty-First School for short –

MARILYN (*sharp*): Yes, yes –

ANDERSON (*remaining unruffled*): And they went on to say we had received a description of the collection of photographs from the previous owner – and the *valuable* pictures which we understand are kept in a separate room, we would dispose of those ourselves . . .

MARILYN*'s eyes flash.*

ANDERSON: And the rest of the collection – separate buyers should be sought for different sections – and we left that up to *you*.

Silence.

MARILYN (*stunned*): You can't split up the collection.

ANDERSON: Ms Truman.

MARILYN: You cannot, you simply *cannot* split up the collection. First you say it is to be closed, and then you tell me it is to be split up. There is no way I can allow that to happen. It is unique, I . . .

ANDERSON: We have to be realistic here.

MARILYN: I *am* being realistic. That is precisely what I'm being. And I'm telling you there is no way that can happen.

ANDERSON's mobile phone rings, it is lying on the desk next to him. He reaches for it.

MARILYN: Don't take that call please.

ANDERSON switches off the phone.

ANDERSON: I have to be on the other side of the site in a few minutes. I have a meeting . . .

MARILYN: A few minutes . . . that's all I've got.

She sits for the first time.

MARILYN: How many is a few minutes?

ANDERSON: How many? Say five.

GARNETT: At the outside. Five at the outside.

MARILYN: Five minutes . . .

Out of the corner of her eye through her office window she can see two cars drawing up on the grass behind the house. Dark-suited men spill out, architects, and site-control management. Through the rest of the scene they pace around outside, surveying the back of the house.

MARILYN: Five minutes is not very long for . . . (*She is trying very hard to keep composed and not let them see her cracking in any way.*) You know to plan the future – it's not that long . . . I'm not very used to time pressures like that.

ANDERSON (*seeing she is affected*): Ms Truman, I understand that this mix-up of communication – let's leave aside for a moment how it happened – I realise that it has come as a shock . . .

15

MARILYN: It certainly is a shock!

OSWALD appears in the aisles of the collection, seen through the open door behind MARILYN's head.

ANDERSON notices him, as OSWALD peers towards them and disappears. This happens as ANDERSON says the following speech.

ANDERSON: But I can only say it is not how we wished it, this is not of our making, we tried to give as much warning as we could.

MARILYN: Well, I'm not going to just sit here sounding outraged – because that is clearly not getting us anywhere. I will merely say what you have outlined is not an option – splitting the collection. It will *never* happen while I'm around. So we will have to sit down calmly and work out an alternative home for the collection in a sensible fashion.

ANDERSON: Ms Truman . . .

He hesitates, looking at her.

MARILYN: If you're waiting for me to say 'Please call me Marilyn' – (*Sharp.*) You'll forgive me but I'm not going to say that . . . Let's keep this as formal as we can. (*Suddenly it flashes out of her.*) The idea that it is OUR FAULT – although I said I wasn't going to sound outraged – that is outrageous!

Again MARILYN notices the men outside the window, one of them on the phone. Then ANDERSON's mobile phone begins to ring.

ANDERSON: Ms Truman . . . the situation – I think it is a little starker than maybe you realise.

MARILYN: I don't see how that is possible. (*Sharp laugh.*) I don't see how that can be the case!

GARNETT (*quietly*): I'm afraid it is possible.

He has taken out his laptop. And through the rest of the scene, he is typing notes as ANDERSON speaks. MARILYN keeps catching sight of his fingers remorselessly typing away.

ANDERSON (*his tone grave*): The situation is this – these buildings are being stripped out, completely rebuilt, that *has* to start in four days' time if we're to have a chance of meeting our schedule. And naturally it has to start on the ground floor of the site. Do you understand what this means, Ms Truman?

He looks across at her.

It means all these rooms have to be empty. I was expecting, when I arrived here today, to see everything packed up, and on the way out.

On this timescale clearly there's absolutely no chance of finding buyers for whole sections of the collection.

MARILYN (*watching beadily*): No chance, *no*.

ANDERSON (*slowly*): The brutal facts are, if I remember the figures correctly – the handful of valuable pictures are worth about 400,000 pounds sterling that is – and the whole rest of the collection, you'd be lucky if you got 160,000 pounds, that is if you could sell every single picture . . . And to even get that price would take months, if not a year.

We move in slowly on MARILYN *as* ANDERSON *tells her what is going to happen.*

ANDERSON: The hard economics are, Ms Truman, that £160,000 is a mere fraction of what even a few days delay on this site would cost. And the cost of storage elsewhere for such a huge collection is of course enormous.

So we'll take the valuable pictures . . . and all the rest will have to be disposed of.

He hesitates for a second, then decides to make it totally clear.

ANDERSON: They will have to be destroyed.

Silence.

MARILYN*'s face impassive, she is sitting in the corner.*

ANDERSON: Clearly, it gives me no pleasure to say this . . .

17

that goes without saying. (*He looks at her.*) Ms Truman?
MARILYN *doesn't react.* GARNETT*'s phone rings, he
mumbles into it to terminate the conversation, says he will
ring the caller back.*

ANDERSON: Ms Truman?

MARILYN: I've said I don't accept it, I can't let it happen . . .
and that had no effect whatsoever.

So . . . I am thinking . . . I am desperately thinking of
how to . . . of what to do. At this precise moment, at this
absolute precise moment – I haven't a clue . . . I can't
really believe you've just said what you have. I mean just
a few minutes ago, literally a few minutes ago, I was
greeting you, everything was sunny, and we were about
to make a great fuss of you.

*She stops. She doesn't know what to do. She is trying very
hard not to break down.*

ANDERSON: Yes, well, I have to say, I've never encountered
this situation before . . . in twenty-five years . . . where
people have carried on regardless in the face of closure . . .
And the effect is devastating . . . clearly . . . When
communications were acknowledged, but nothing stirred.

MARILYN: Nothing stirred . . . (*She looks around.*) What
sleepy people we must appear.

She looks across at him. For a moment their eyes meet

MARILYN: Just to show we're not completely dopey – I want
one thing.

ANDERSON: And what is that?

MARILYN: I want you to see the collection.

ANDERSON: Well – of course that would be interesting –
but I have a schedule . . . which –

MARILYN: I really think you should see the collection –
before you destroy it.

ANDERSON: Ms Truman, *I* didn't cause the situation, I wish
it was other than it is, but I will *not* be made to feel –

MARILYN (*quickly*): That was crass of me – I'm sorry (*She*

18

tries to smile.) I was just getting somewhere – and then I
said that! You'll come and see the collection, after your
big meeting? Come on, what have you got to lose? (*She
stares at him.*) A quick walk?

ANDERSON: A quick walk . . . maybe, but I need to know,
do you accept the situation?

MARILYN: I want you to see the collection.

ANDERSON: Ms Truman – I don't want to sound like a
lawyer . . . but you must tell me you accept the
situation.

MARILYN: I accept we have a problem.

ANDERSON: *No*, I need to know you understand what's
happening. That the library is closing.

MARILYN: I'll understand – if you come and see the
collection.

Suddenly ANDERSON *and* GARNETT *sweep out.*

ANDERSON (*as he leaves*): We'll call with a time . . . it will
have to be in the next three hours.

OSWALD *is standing outside the door to greet them in the
passage, he is smoking a little cigar.*

OSWALD: Ready for a drink now, everyone?!

INT. THE CAFETERIA. DAY.

MARILYN, OSWALD, VERONICA SPIG *and* NICK *are
sitting at a formal dining-table eating lunch.* OSWALD *at one
end of the table drinking red wine.* MARILYN *at the other end
sitting very straight, quiet, contained. The dinner ladies are
fussing around. There is a sense of a daily ritual being observed.
They are deep into the first course, melon and Parma ham.*

OSWALD: They would be appalled, absolutely appalled if
they could see this – a full sit-down service! Only the five
of us!

VERONICA: I'm sure if we do our best to be reasonable . . .

19

if we do our *very* best . . . they will see sense.

SPIG: No way. It's just business to them. They are killers. By the end of the day – we'll be finished.

OSWALD (*staring down the table*): Marilyn will handle it – you'll see. (MARILYN *is eating very small pieces.*) Besides I have a plan.

VERONICA: You do?

OSWALD: I do and it's simple. We should still be here eating lunch when they arrive.

NICK: That's a plan?!

OSWALD: Very much so. (*He sips his wine.*) A surprisingly good plan.

SPIG *rolls her eyes as* OSWALD *cuts into his Parma ham.*

OSWALD: No – contrary to appearances I'm serious. If we're still here, eating a formal meal, it will suggest instantly that they are dealing with irrational people.

With crazies! (*Filling his glass.*) They will think 'What do these guys do when faced with the biggest crisis of their lives?! – They have a five-course lunch . . . as if nothing has happened!' That will be very alarming.

SPIG: Oh yeah?!

OSWALD: Yeah . . . The one thing any business dreads dealing with is people that don't respond to any rules.

That don't show enough fear – which we won't. The characters we're dealing with need fear. Everything in their life is fear, deadlines, hirings, firings – all fear. Remove fear from the equation and you're saying, 'I don't care, I'm facing extinction *but I don't care.*'

Then they will get worried, they'll start thinking – 'These arseholes could do anything, they could set fire to the building if they wanted.' (*He beams.*) Which clearly we could! So our American friends will decide 'We must be much more careful, give these guys a lot more time.' (*He smiles down the table.*) So I've taken the liberty of extending the menu. After the melon . . . (MOLLY *the dinner lady is beaming at them.*) We have a blackcurrant sorbet . . . then some corn on the cob . . . then a roast.

NICK (*grins*): We're going to eat our way to victory?!

OSWALD: Can't think of any better way!

MARILYN: Oswald . . . can I have a word?

OSWALD *looks up with a piece of Parma ham dangling from his mouth.*

OSWALD: Absolutely. Maybe between the third and fourth courses?

INT. MARILYN'S OFFICE. DAY.

Afternoon sunlight creating strong shadows. OSWALD *is sitting in the window seat, with some corn on the cob awash with melted butter on his plate.*

MARILYN (*staring across at him*): So?

OSWALD (*very relaxed*): So?

MARILYN: Oswald . . . they're coming back pretty shortly, and however hard I keep thinking – it's clear if I don't have any cards to play, that is going to be that.

OSWALD: You don't agree with my analysis? With my eating offensive?

MARILYN: Be serious, Oswald, please.

OSWALD (*wiping the butter with a napkin*): Well, I *was* making a serious point. (*He looks at her.*) We have two choices, and *only* two. Do something truly perverse, which makes them doubt our sanity –

MARILYN *stares across at the large slopping figure of* OSWALD, *with his napkin tucked into his neck. She smiles.*

MARILYN: Maybe we don't have to work too hard at that . . .

OSWALD: – which is the choice as you know I favour . . . and though you don't believe me there are many successful historical precedents – at the battle of Austerlitz for instance some Austrian deserters sat down in the middle of the battlefield and started having lunch, while under fire, a picnic! They escaped the firing squad quite easily, because of insanity –

MARILYN: What's the second choice, Oswald?

OSWALD (*turning the corn on the cob over*): Play dirty.

MARILYN: How?

OSWALD *gets up, suddenly a piercing look in his eyes.*

OSWALD: There's only one thing that interests those guys – and that of course is money. (*He stops moving and grins.*) Sex too probably . . . but I'm not sure Spig is up to it . . .

MARILYN: Go on.

OSWALD: So it's extremely simple. Blindingly obvious in fact. We have a few very valuable pictures – so instead of leaving them locked up very conveniently in a little room for the Americans to come along and collect . . . We sprinkle them away among the collection . . . We 'lose' them in all the other pictures – you try finding them among ten million photographs, if you don't know where to look! It'd be like trying to find the right piece of hay in a haystack. They'll never do it!

MARILYN: You mean – 'You give us more time to find a home for the collection – or you don't ever find the pictures'?

OSWALD: You got it in one!

MARILYN: It's blackmail.

OSWALD: Of course. (*He smiles.*) And isn't that great?! . . . It's the only language they understand.

INT. STRONG ROOM. DAY.
We cut to a windowless room with red walls, OSWALD *and* MARILYN *handling the valuable photos: a Man Ray, Brassai, Kertesz; stunning pictures.*

OSWALD: So our prize fish the Man Ray – probably go for

£120,000 . . . where shall we put it . . . ? Among the Woolworth's shop-fronts of the 1950s?

OSWALD *is taking the precious photos out of their fine individual boxes, where they are covered with delicate tracing paper. He is putting them in a series of ordinary brown boxes with grubby old labels.*

MARILYN: If I was in Mr Anderson's position and somebody did this – I would immediately lose all respect for them, at a stroke.

OSWALD: You think he respects us!?

MARILYN: He could be made to.

OSWALD: You're out of your mind – he thinks we're pathetic dusty people, who stepped straight out of an Ealing comedy with Margaret Rutherford! That's what he thinks – we're bumbling prats!

(*He stares at her.*) So these prats have to sink their teeth – into his fleshy parts. (*With feeling.*) That is the *only* thing prats like us can do.

MARILYN: It would irritate me, it would enrage me – if this was done to me.

OSWALD: We *want* to enrage him.

MARILYN: I'm not sure, I don't think we'll ever prevail being this childish – things don't work like that.

OSWALD (*challengingly*): Where don't they work like that?

MARILYN: Outside . . . out there.

OSWALD: 'Out there'! . . . What do you know about that?! You go out and about even less than I do . . . !

(*Loud.*) Do you want the collection to be saved or not . . . ?

Pause.

MARILYN (*reluctantly*): It *might* buy us time . . . (*She moves.*) But I'm also not sure he won't just destroy the collection, with these inside if he can't find them.

OSWALD: He'd have to be crackers to do that . . . ! It would get his whole project terrible publicity. Nobody's going

to torch this place, if they can't find these. I promise
you.

INT. CONSERVATORY. DAY.
MARILYN *is standing with* OSWALD *at the doors of the
collection.* VERONICA *and* NICK *standing close by.*

They are watching ANDERSON *and* GARNETT *walking
towards them briskly, being escorted by* SPIG. *They begin to
move across the cafeteria towards* MARILYN.

MARILYN *(calling across)*: In a hurry?
ANDERSON: You think I'm always in a hurry?
MARILYN: So how long have I got this time?
ANDERSON *(calmly)*: I said I'd look at the collection in
    exchange for your understanding and accepting the
    situation. And this is what we'll do.
GARNETT: We'll be taking calls and doing all the business
    we need to here. Everything is under control.
OSWALD *(smiles)*: You think? That's reassuring.
    ANDERSON. *leans against a chair. His manner is
    disconcertingly relaxed.*
ANDERSON: And before we plunge in – I have an
    announcement – for the employees here. (*He glances at
    the five of them.*) We will be conducting interviews to see
    if we can employ you elsewhere. In the administrative
    section of our new project . . . so nobody need be out of
    a job – subject to interview of course.
SPIG: So it means nothing – (*She mimics.*) Because it's
    'subject to interview' . . .
ANDERSON *(grins at* SPIG): I'm sure you can handle it . . .
    (*He stares at them.*) So we all understand that? (*Indicates
    doors.*) Let's go and take a look then.

INT. GROUND FLOOR HALL COLLECTION. DAY.
*For the first time we move inside the collection. Compared to the
rest of the building there's much less light. As far as we can see
stretch row upon row of shelves packed tight with boxes of photos.
Elsewhere files of photos are suspended floating, on wire shelves,
hanging in slightly ghostly lines. The first thing we see on entering
the collection, is a series of photos outside their boxes, that have
been displayed by* OSWALD *and* MARILYN *for inspection by
their visitors.*

INT. VERONICA'S COLLECTION. DAY.
*Beautiful images of a crowd completely hidden by a mass of black
umbrellas. A child standing in front of a totally ruined palace,
horses plunging through gunfire, a girl waving to a boat,
disappearing into a haze on an Italian lake.*

*The pictures keep coming at us, and for a moment we give over
to their intense beauty – just as* ANDERSON *does. We move
from the pictures to* ANDERSON'S *watchful gaze, and then to*
MARILYN *studying his every reaction – as she wills the
photographs to work their magic on him.*

VERONICA *appears beside* MARILYN, *her face anxious,
hoping* ANDERSON *is being affected.*

The sequence is brought to an abrupt end by OSWALD. *His
voice cuts in loudly.*

OSWALD (*in a loud American accent*): OK you guys, let's start
    firing!
ANDERSON: Firing? What do you mean? Nobody's firing
    anybody.

INT. OSWALD'S COLLECTION. DAY.
OSWALD *is standing in the middle·of one of the aisles,
surrounded by shelves, staring back at* ANDERSON *like a*

gunfighter down the length of the room. MARILYN *is standing next to* ANDERSON. VERONICA, SPIG *and* NICK *are following at a safe distance.*

OSWALD: No, no fire away! At me. I'll find anything you want – within seven seconds . . .

ANDERSON: Seven seconds?

OSWALD: Too long? Seven seconds is quite long you're right, we'll make it five.

GARNETT: I take it you're computerised.

OSWALD (*his voice rising in astonishment*): You think we have computers in here! – it'll take years to catalogue all this and get it on line . . . of course we have no computers, it's all in here. (*He taps his forehead.*)

OK, shoot – since the word fire makes you nervous. Shoot *now* . . . What do you want? (*Before they can reply.*) The giant squid? – always goes down well! . . . It is widely believed nobody has ever photographed the giant squid alive and under water – but we have a picture here, taken fifty years ago – of precisely that! Want to see the giant squid?

ANDERSON: I think we'll pass on the giant squid.

OSWALD (*ignoring this*): Some people think it's a fake, just a run-of-the-mill calamari held close to the camera, that's why it's not world-famous – but I personally feel it's the real giant, caught in all its glorious murkiness. Want me to find it?

ANDERSON: I think it would be a better test, wouldn't it – if *we* nominated the subject.

OSWALD: Yes. Of course! That's what I meant. (*He smiles.*) I was just a little overeager to show the squid. Shoot.

ANDERSON: You probably wouldn't have a picture . . . but my home town Emporia in Virginia.

OSWALD: That's too easy.

ANDERSON: It's not that easy – it's not a very big town.

OSWALD: I tell you it's too easy.

ANDERSON: OK . . . our street then . . . Limone Avenue . . .
you won't have that.

Before ANDERSON *has finished the sentence,* OSWALD's
*bulky shape has launched off amongst the shelves moving
with surprising speed. He gives a great leap to get a box
down from a high shelf, a few other boxes tumble down as
well, as he dislodges them with his leap, but he comes
powering back, with a box open, a whirl of photographs
inside. And there is the town.*

OSWALD: Here it is, Emporia.

ANDERSON: Jesus . . . there it is, yes.

OSWALD: And then . . . (*He makes a special effects sort of
noise.*) we get closer, just like a computer blow-up . . . we
zoom, we zoom closer . . . the main street of Emporia
(*He produces another photo.*) and then . . . (*He produces
the next picture with a triumphant flourish.*)

The corner of Chestnut Tree Avenue and Limone
Avenue.

ANDERSON *is genuinely impressed.*

ANDERSON (*soft whistle*): Just look at that . . . !

OSWALD: Yes . . . a sleepy place . . . a sleepy time.

*We see a small town street at cherry-blossom time. It looks
like the late fifties judging by the cars.*

OSWALD: So you were there then? (*He smiles.*) Do you see
yourself?

The camera searches the windows of the photograph, as
ANDERSON *studies it.*

OSWALD: Your little head sticking out? Your little freckled
face . . . ? (*Suddenly it flashes out of him.*) Somewhere
you're there, saying – 'Hey, Dad, let's go and close the
local museum, it's not worth shit!'

ANDERSON (*immediately gives the picture back*): Yes – well,
thanks for finding that –

MARILYN (*moving sharply*): Come on, everyone, there's a lot to see . . .

OSWALD: How long was that? We didn't get an official
timing . . . for finding the picture. (*As they move.*) So,
shoot again, anybody!

GARNETT: Shall we see the prime collection? The really
valuable pictures?

MARILYN (*quickly*): Yes – but maybe before we go there,
you would like to see our portrait section . . . ?

OSWALD: No, no, that's boring . . . !

He pushes ahead of them.

INT. OSWALD'S ROOM. DAY.
OSWALD *staring at us.*

OSWALD (*smiles*): And it gets worse too . . .
He takes a photo and the flash takes us back to them in the
passage coming towards us.

INT. PASSAGE IN COLLECTION. DAY.

OSWALD: No, no, much more unexpected is this –
He opens a little side door.

INT. BASEMENT EROTICA ROOM. DAY.
They move into a darkened chamber, OSWALD *beams as they*
enter.

OSWALD: Our erotica . . . (*Turning slowly in the room.*)
Mostly Victorian and Edwardian erotica.

MARILYN (*trying to make the best of* OSWALD *bringing them*
in): There are some very beautiful pictures, in one of
these drawers.

OSWALD: Some naughty snaps from the twenties too!

> ANDERSON *is discomfited suddenly, confronted by these faded naked figures.*

ANDERSON: It feels rather sad in here. (*He glances around.*) A lot of yearning –

OSWALD (*surprised by this*): That's good. Yes. (*Shots of Edwardian erotica.*) Yearning. (*He grins.*) Something I know all about!

> ANDERSON *shifting uneasily, not sure if* OSWALD *is about to go into personal details.* VERONICA'*s sharp bird-like face glancing closely at the erotica.*

OSWALD: You want to see our images of obsession? Obsession is always interesting, isn't it?! (*He takes a folder out from a special drawer.*) A rather plump nude woman from a seaside resort, 1910, photographed in an astonishing series of poses and interesting positions . . .

ANDERSON (*hastily moving*): Shall we move on – I want to see the great pictures.

> OSWALD *butts in before* MARILYN *can say anything.*

OSWALD: That's easy . . .

> OSWALD *leads on, moving purposefully among the shelves and opens another small door.*

OSWALD: Here we are, the strong room.

INT. BASEMENT COLLECTION. STRONG ROOM. DAY.
We move inside the room with the red walls, now denuded of pictures.

OSWALD (*mock surprise*) Oh . . . ! Goodness me! . . . They have gone!

MARILYN (*quickly*): They were moved a few months ago – to other parts of the collection, for security reasons.

GARNETT (*disbelief*): For security reasons – you moved them *out* of the strong room?!

MARILYN: Yes, there have been various burglaries of other collections, where they lost all their best pictures, because they were so easy to find.

ANDERSON: So why were we brought in here then?

OSWALD: To whet your appetite! (*He suddenly moves off.*) So what next . . . ? (*He moves to another shelf.*) How about shop-fronts . . . ?! We've got a fine collection of Woolworth's from the 1950s . . . !

ANDERSON *and* GARNETT *move in the other direction,* GARNETT *rolling his eyes to* ANDERSON.

ANDERSON (*turns away from the blank wall to* MARILYN): I think we'd better have a word –

OSWALD (*calling after them*): Not interested in the shop-fronts . . . ? (*Then, out of the corner of his mouth, to* MARILYN.) They'll never look at those again now!

ANDERSON *who has moved ahead, stops and calls* MARILYN.

ANDERSON: I think we'd better have a word – now!

INT. OSWALD'S COLLECTION. DAY.

They move outside, back among the shelves of the main collection. The others watch from the doorway, catching glimpses of them among the hanging photos.

We cut between ANDERSON *and* MARILYN, *their faces close, and* OSWALD*'s POV, watching them at a distance from the doorway.*

ANDERSON (*his voice lowered*): You know, Ms Truman – if I was to believe that those pictures have been moved today, distributed among all the other photos – so we can't find them . . .

If I was to believe that –

MARILYN: That has not happened.

ANDERSON: If I was to believe that – I would form a truly

low opinion of whoever had done that.

MARILYN (*staring straight back at him*): I would never do something as crude as that. You will get your pictures.

ANDERSON: So let's see them.

MARILYN: You will see them.

ANDERSON: Now . . . ?

MARILYN: Any moment . . . I want you to be able to appreciate the full collection.

ANDERSON: I have seen the collection.

MARILYN: No you haven't. You haven't even begun . . . There are all sorts of things here – all kinds of pictures . . . with the most incredible stories attached.

Where we are right now, for instance . . . where we're standing . . . within three feet of us – there's six or seven hair-raising things . . .

Her hand goes up hovering over the boxes of pictures.

MARILYN: Like . . . here . . .

ANDERSON: Do you know the contents of every box – without even reading the label?

MARILYN (*smiles*): Not every one . . . no . . . So – in here . . . (*Brings the box carefully down so it is close to* ANDERSON*'s face.*) They are the three fat brothers who committed a very bizarre murder – with apples and a crossbow – the William Tell murder.

ANDERSON *restraining her hand as she opens the box.*

ANDERSON (*firmly*): Ms Truman, I've explained the situation – and you've agreed and accepted it. However hard you try to weave a spell – that won't alter anything.

MARILYN: You don't want to hear the stories?

ANDERSON: I've got time for *one*.

MARILYN: Just one? I thought you had all the time it took . . .

ANDERSON: I've got the time for one.

MARILYN *stares down the long aisle of shelves.*

MARILYN: A million pictures – one story? . . . Out of all that?

31

ANDERSON: Some challenge, eh?

    MARILYN *looks straight at him.*

MARILYN: Right! (*Their eyes meet.*)

INT. TALL WINDOWLESS ROOM. DAY.

A stark room with a high ceiling and no windows, the walls have big scars of green paint. A trestle table is in the middle of the room, and an anglepoise light is shining.

    MARILYN *is sitting on one side of the table,* ANDERSON *on the other.* MARILYN *has in front of her a series of identical thin, plain brown boxes, which she is moving around slowly, like moving playing cards.*

ANDERSON (*in mid-sentence*): . . . you know what I really don't like about today is how suddenly I'm the villain of all this. How I'm made out to be no better than any number-crunching moron who comes marching in and says flush the whole thing down the waste disposal right now – that really annoys me . . . In fact you know nothing about me . . .

    MARILYN'*s eyes flick. She looks up from the table sensing she's making a connection.*

MARILYN: No I don't. You're right. (*Slight smile.*) Why don't you tell me . . . ?

ANDERSON (*smiles, seeing through this*): I think we'll leave that for another time.

MARILYN: But I thought there wasn't going to be another time?

ANDERSON: Not another time like this, no.

    He stares at a message on his pager for a second.

    What I find really strange is – I've been forced into having to take this position because of incompetence at *your end* – the negligence of Mr Oswald Bates – but *nobody* seems to mention that! (*Glancing at* MARILYN.)

And what's more, what we're doing with the Twenty-
First School suddenly becomes like we're just putting up
a piece of cheap real estate, yet another hotel or car-park
or something, instead of what we're actually doing –
which is planning a really progressive educational
establishment.

MARILYN (*simply*): A *business* school.

ANDERSON: A unique outfit – which is not just another way
of making money.

MARILYN: Good. (*Slight smile.*) I'm glad you're not just
making money. That's reassuring . . .

ANDERSON: And then what do you do? – On top of all this!
. . . You disappear the most important pictures! And so
we have to act like in a children's story now – like the bad
guys in *Tom Thumb* – I refuse to be that, I'm not going
round shaking people saying, 'Where are the pictures –?!
Get me the pictures . . . !'

MARILYN: Right. (*Innocently.*) So you're not saying give me
the pictures, any more?

ANDERSON (*watching her*): I'm not going to say it – but I'm
not leaving today without them . . .

MARILYN *is impassive.*

There is a knock on the large heavy door and SPIG *comes
in with a jug of orange juice and two glasses.*

SPIG: Thought you could do with this. (*To* ANDERSON, *as
she places it on the table.*) Help you survive. (*She smiles
and begins to leave.*) Because you'll need it.

ANDERSON (*as* SPIG *shuts the door behind her*): What's
going to happen here?

MARILYN *pushes the first brown box in front of her, it lies
between the two of them on the table.*

MARILYN: Just a story.

ANDERSON *watches* MARILYN *lift the lid off the box.*

ANDERSON: It's not a horror story? There's not going to be
body parts . . . Trying to shock?

MARILYN: Certainly not. (*Indicating pager and mobile.*) All
electronics off please.

ANDERSON: But . . .

MARILYN: All of them *off*.

ANDERSON *switches his phone off.*

MARILYN: It's important to watch closely –
*She drops a picture of a child on to the table. A little girl of
about seven, dressed in thirties clothes.*

ANDERSON: A little girl?

MARILYN: A little girl . . . yes.

ANDERSON: Going for the heart strings then?

MARILYN: I hope so.
*She takes out more images of the girl, all portrait pictures of
her.*

MARILYN: A little Jewish girl. Lily Katzman. In Berlin –

ANDERSON: Jewish too? . . . A Holocaust story? (*Softly.*) It
won't be difficult to move me . . . I get affected very
quickly by those stories . . . You've taken an easy route.

MARILYN: Don't jump to conclusions.
We see a whole spread of Lily's portraits across the table.

MARILYN: Lily Katzman was the daughter of a doctor who
was also an amateur photographer –
*We see various full-length pictures of the young girl posed
against a curtain.*

MARILYN: And her father made many studies of her . . . he
worshipped her with his camera.
She brushes away the portraits, moves them to one side.

MARILYN: The persecution of the Jews starts of course . . .
the family split up. The mother and father go into
hiding . . .
*We see an image of a stiff formal family group, of a rich
family, grandmother, father, mother and their children.*

MARILYN: Somehow Lily becomes part of this household,
this family – because she doesn't look too Jewish. The
Oelendorff's adopted her – a rich upper-bourgeois

family, one little girl appears in their midst, explained away no doubt as a distant niece . . .

We close in on the elderly grandmother.

MARILYN: The matriarch of the family probably wasn't aware what was really going on.

We see contemporary photographs of rich, heavily furnished thirties interiors, the camera moving very close into the photographs. The rooms are empty.

Then we see a picture of Lily standing on her own, by a very ornate clock.

MARILYN (*her voice quiet*): A very unusual situation in itself, this rich, completely conventional merchant family, harbouring this Jewish child – putting the whole family at great risk . . . Nobody knows why it happened.

We search the faces of the family.

A love child? . . . A secret affair? . . . Or were they being brave in a way that so few others were? . . .

ANDERSON (*staring at their faces*): Or was there Jewish blood in the family that nobody outside guessed at . . . ?

We move in among the photos of the rooms of the mansion.

MARILYN: Lily is not allowed out of the house, though she is allowed to greet visitors. (*She reaches for another box.*) But then one day . . . it is arranged for her to see her parents.

Close-up of ANDERSON.

MARILYN: They are in hiding, living in a basement room, in a house on the other side of the city.

The plan is for her to meet her father first at some halfway point, . . . and then he will take her to a public park to meet her mother.

MARILYN *stares at* ANDERSON.

MARILYN: They meet –

ANDERSON: They do? . . .

MARILYN: Yes. But her father . . . when he sees her . . . he wants to buy her something.

ANDERSON: Buy her something? . . . That's a risk – that's dangerous surely . . . ?

MARILYN: He wants to give her a present. His daughter. He doesn't know when he'll see her again. The most natural thing in the world . . . He takes these pictures of her, on the street . . .

We begin to see the sequence of pictures of Lily on the broad pavements of wartime Berlin.

MARILYN: As Lily window-shops . . . looking for something to buy . . . They try to seem as normal as possible . . . Trying not to move too quickly, not seem too rushed, just a father with his daughter . . . taking pictures.

ANDERSON: But her mother is waiting . . . They have to reach her –

MARILYN: Yes. They must have been so acutely aware of time . . . Maybe they didn't buy anything after all because of that –

We see a picture of the mother sitting alone in a long dress on a bench.

ANDERSON: There she is . . . So they do meet in the park –

MARILYN: Yes . . . Their last meeting –

ANDERSON's *eyes flick.*

MARILYN: Her papa records the moment.

We see the mother sitting in a long dress, on a bench in the park. First sitting by herself, then a picture of Lily approaching the bench, and a third picture of them sitting side by side.

MARILYN: They meet in the park . . . their last meeting. These pictures . . . her papa took these pictures. Their few minutes together . . . as the Berliners promenade around them in the park.

We see stills of Berliners in a park, laughing faces, people wheeling prams, or talking in little clusters.

MARILYN: Then something happens in the park.

We see more faces in the park, Berliners eating a picnic etc.

MARILYN: We don't know what happens . . . but the mother

decides they must leave immediately . . . she goes first –
We see the park, the mother glimpsed on a gravel path,
turned towards us, a grainy picture, she is some distance
away from us.

We see the Berliners faces again.

We go back to the path, the mother is a receding figure
now, her back turned towards us.

MARILYN: The last time she saw her mother.

ANDERSON: Who survived this story? Who wrote it down?
Did Lily? . . . Did her father?

MARILYN: You have to listen – you have to wait . . .
She opens another box and spreads more pictures before us.

MARILYN: Her father takes a couple of final pictures . . .
Lily looks strained, staring back at us standing next to a
fountain.

MARILYN: Then he leaves . . .

ANDERSON: He leaves her there? Alone in the park?

MARILYN: It was safer that way – it had been arranged that
somebody from the Oelendorffs would pick her up. But
nobody comes.
We see more pictures of Berliners in cafés, moving in a park,
a bandstand with a band playing, people eating cake.

ANDERSON (*getting very involved*): So is she arrested then?
Is she arrested in the park? He shouldn't have left her –
We see again the picture of Lily, the last one her father took.

MARILYN: She decides to go . . . Lily decides to leave the
park – to find her own way home . . .
She pushes another brown box along the table, and takes off
the lid.

MARILYN: These are more pictures of Berlin at the time . . .
We see broad peaceful streets, we see people in fine coats,
exercising their dogs.

MARILYN: We know she goes into a chemist's shop like this
one . . . to ask directions.
We see the rich interior of a chemist's shop with its huge glass

37

jars, the camera moving slowly across the photograph,
looking at the bottles and the people behind the counter.

ANDERSON: Do they betray her?

MARILYN: Lily moves along the streets.

We see another strasse.

She loses her way again, and she goes into a bank, to ask more directions.

We see a rather magnificent bank interior of the period, with Berliners smartly dressed, making financial transactions.

ANDERSON: She wanders in there? . . . A little girl in the bank . . . on her own?! They're bound to be suspicious . . . why did she go in there? If she had just asked on the street –

MARILYN: She did go into a bank and she did ask directions – but she got frightened while waiting and ran away.

ANDERSON: But somebody took the address, right? That she had asked for . . . they were waiting when she got home?

MARILYN: She left the bank . . . (*She moves to another box.*) And then . . . you must realise these pictures are from all over the collection. (*She lifts the contents out of the box.*) And this is the most extraordinary thing – totally by coincidence, an official photographer, a Nazi photographer, was taking photos of a parade.

We see routine pictures of a Nazi parade and the crowd watching.

And he was also taking pictures of the crowd.

We see photos of an adoring crowd waving flags, various different faces of the period.

MARILYN: And he unwittingly takes a picture of Lily . . . of her journey home . . . because she came upon the parade and had to stand waiting for it to pass. So we can see her trying to get home.

We see a group of four people waving flags, a tight group of enthusiastic faces, and in among them we see Lily's small figure, her face looking sideways.

ANDERSON: There she is . . . remarkable! How did you find this picture?

MARILYN: Oswald found it of course. When we were given her father's pictures, Oswald went through every still we had of Berlin, of that period – and there are a lot of those – in case there was something else of her. It took him ages. But he found her.

ANDERSON: Where now people would study security videos to see if anybody had been caught on camera –

MARILYN: Exactly! There by an amazing chance is Lily – on part of her dangerous journey home . . . halfway there . . .

ANDERSON (*anxious to know*): And did she get home?

MARILYN: She got home yes. But the Oelendorffs were questioned that very afternoon. The whole family was arrested . . . even the matriarch.
We move in on the grandmother's face.

MARILYN: And Lily too of course . . .
We see shots of late thirties Berlin moving about its business, unconcerned.

ANDERSON: And are there any other pictures? Or does the trail go cold there? It can't go cold! . . . There's more?
MARILYN *reaches for another box.*

MARILYN: Oswald went through everything, all the shots we have of Jewish people being rounded up, the trains, the stations, the cattle trucks, the lorries, every image we have like that in the collection . . .
Close-up of ANDERSON.

ANDERSON: And he found her?

MARILYN: And he eventually found this . . .
We see an extremely affecting picture of a uniformed German guard, standing with his back to us, and in front of him are five children in a neat row, crossing some railway tracks, each carrying a small suitcase.

Lily is the last in line, staring straight at the camera.

ANDERSON (*very affected*): Their little suitcases . . .

MARILYN: Those little suitcases, yes I know . . .

ANDERSON: It goes on then? From them on the train?
Where is the next picture? Did Oswald find any more?

MARILYN: No more pictures like that, no . . .

She moves to the final box.

MARILYN: But there is this . . . (*She opens the box.*)

ANDERSON (*waving his hand*): Please . . . if it's a pile of
those bodies, I know we can't change history here, but
I'd rather not see it . . . I can imagine too well.

MARILYN: No – Lily did survive –

ANDERSON: She did!

MARILYN: It was her son-in-law that brought us her father's
pictures . . . and from what he told us, and from a tiny
passport photo that he showed Oswald, from that
evidence – Oswald stared at all the pictures we had of
street scenes round the Elephant and Castle and Old
Kent Road, here in London.

ANDERSON: She's in this city?!

MARILYN: All the pictures we had from the sixties, seventies
and eighties . . . and again he found her . . . here is Lily
. . . in the Old Kent Road in 1987.

*We see a startlingly upsetting picture of a fat woman,
looking far older than her years dressed like a bag lady,
indeed she is carrying a clump of bags, and she is screaming
across at somebody who we can't see in the picture in a mad,
contorted raging sort of way.*

ANDERSON (*staring at the picture*) That's not her – that's not
Lily.

MARILYN: That *is* Lily. I promise you. it's been confirmed.

*We move from the image of the fat bag lady, caught in the
middle of a paranoid rant, over to the pictures of a young
Lily looking radiant in her father's pictures . . . and then over
to the picture of the little children crossing the railway line*

with their suitcases. And then back to ANDERSON *who is visibly moved. He picks up the pictures and spreads them in chronological order, her whole story in a line in front of him.*

ANDERSON: You showed me these – you told me this particular story because these pictures came from all over the collection. Right? . . . A twentieth-century tale, caught like that.

MARILYN *watches* ANDERSON *as he is staring at the pictures. She has affected him she realises, but she doesn't know how much.* ANDERSON *gets up suddenly, starts pacing in the tall windowless room.*

ANDERSON: Marilyn . . . I'm going to start calling you that – because even after a few hours Ms Truman doesn't seem right . . . Marilyn –

MARILYN *watching.*

ANDERSON: I cannot change my decision. You understand. It *is* a bad situation . . . it is very unfortunate – but it cannot be changed. The economics of the situation prevent it.

MARILYN*'s eyes flicker.*

ANDERSON: Moreover, you have our pictures, you have 'stolen' if you like £400,000 worth of photos . . .

MARILYN: Not stolen –

ANDERSON: Give those back . . .

MARILYN: – You will have them back.

ANDERSON: Give them back now – and you can have a deal. You can take anything you want from the collection . . . anything you can house or store yourself, you can have it – for *free*.

Fill bags and bags of it if you want . . . a truckload!

You do that because *you know* what's important, where the pictures worth preserving are.

MARILYN: I will *not* split up the collection.

ANDERSON: Oh, for goodness sake don't be so proud, Marilyn! – You have miles and miles of routine pictures here . . . of shop-fronts and other crap that's in a thousand other collections. (*Loud.*) Save what is important for Christ's sake! Get to work on it now – use your knowledge . . . save what really matters! . . . You *have* to compromise.

MARILYN: I said I'd never split it up.

ANDERSON: Marilyn – there is simply no alternative. (*He stares at her concerned she makes the right choice.*) Go on – take it . . . (*Pause.*) Take the *deal*.
Silence.

INT. COLLECTION. DAY.
Outside in the passage. SPIG, VERONICA *watching the door anxiously* . . . OSWALD *slightly apart drinking a cup of tea . . . rather fine china.*

INT. TALL WINDOWLESS ROOM. DAY.

MARILYN (*quiet*): You're right. I have to.

ANDERSON (*more gently*): You do, you do have to. Yes.

MARILYN (*suddenly*): *But.*

ANDERSON: But what?

MARILYN: You must keep all the staff on – that want to be here.

ANDERSON: Does that include you?

MARILYN (*calmly*): No. Of course not. But the others . . . you said you would.

ANDERSON: Yes – subject to interview.

MARILYN: You can do that now, today.

ANDERSON (*startled*): Now?!

MARILYN: Yes, see them now – so nobody leaves tonight without a job. (*She stares at him.*) That's the deal.

INT. THE COLLECTION. HALL AREA. EVENING INTO NIGHT.
OSWALD *is standing in the library watching* MARILYN *approaching holding the valuable pictures. The door of her office is half open and* ANDERSON *and* GARNETT *can be glimpsed waiting inside.* ANDERSON *is on the phone.*

OSWALD: Don't do this, Marilyn. (*As she approaches, he indicates the pictures she's carrying.*) These are our big weapon . . . What are you doing handing them back?

MARILYN (*up to him, her voice lowered*): They've served their purpose, I don't think we can play any more games with them –

OSWALD: Games! . . . So you think everything is going to be hunky-dory, after this!? – You think those robots in there are going to stick to their word?

MARILYN: I assure you I'm going to make them.

OSWALD: Oh yeah? . . .

He takes one of the valuable pictures, the Kertesz, stares at it.

MARILYN: And what's more they're not robots –

OSWALD (*muttering*): They've got to you . . . (*Fingering the picture.*) It's odd, isn't it, how much money one or two pictures are worth . . . (*He mimes tearing the picture in two.* MARILYN *carefully takes it off him.*)

MARILYN: Oswald . . .

OSWALD: We should not be co-operating – total non-compliance – that is how we should be fighting. I *promise* you it will work . . .

MARILYN: No, it's time to co-operate. We have to.

OSWALD: You mean like tearing the collection to pieces . . . which you are about to do, wrecking it?!

MARILYN (*with feeling*): We have to salvage something.

She begins to move on, then turns, her face close.

MARILYN: And do me a favour, please, Oswald, when they talk to you – try to be reasonable.

INT. WINDOWLESS ROOM. NIGHT.

We cut to SPIG *facing* GARNETT *in the windowless room. She is eating a bag of crisps and smoking. She is in mid-sentence.*

SPIG: – what skills do I have . . . ?

GARNETT: Yes, what do you think your strengths are?

SPIG (*crunches away for a moment*): Well, working here, you must understand – working here it's different. I can tell you about . . . what can I tell you? . . .

I can tell you for instance how many pictures we've got of alligators being cut open, with human remains inside, coming out of them . . . We have seven of those . . . (*She smiles.*) Not sure that's the sort of skills you mean, is it?

INT. CAFETERIA. NIGHT.

We cut to NICK *facing* ANDERSON *in the darkened cafeteria. He is in precisely the same situation, in mid-sentence. The cafeteria stretches behind him.*

NICK: . . . I don't say very much, you know. I never said much before I came to work here . . . but now I say even less.

ANDERSON: Why is that?

NICK *doesn't react.*

ANDERSON: Do you know why that's happened?

NICK (*looks at him*): I think that's all I have to say on the subject.

INT. WINDOWLESS ROOM. NIGHT.

We cut back to SPIG, *smoking sensually, staring at an uptight* GARNETT.

SPIG: . . . it's amazing how when you're stoned these
    pictures come back to life . . . what patterns form . . . in
    the night! You have no idea what it's like at night . . . I
    mean I know it's dark now . . . but I'm talking very late
    . . . and when you're really *really* stoned – what you
    suddenly see then . . . it's better than the movies . . . it's
    better than telly . . . it's fantastic!

INT. CAFETERIA. NIGHT.
VERONICA *staring straight at us. Her sharp bird-like face
twitching.* ANDERSON *watching.*

VERONICA: I'm afraid there's nothing interesting about me
    at all . . . I just beaver, that's all I do, that's all I've ever
    done, beaver away . . . (*She glances up.*) And usually
    people seem satisfied.

INT. PHOTOGRAPHIC LIBRARY. NIGHT.
We cut to MARILYN *beginning to pull pieces of the collection
out, moving among the shelves. Her face taut. She is splitting up
the collection.*

    *We see images, photographs of groups of girls hoola-hooping,
Catholic priests playing football, a child running towards us with
a traction engine looming up behind him . . .*

    MARILYN *turns away from the shelves moving restlessly on.
Outside the window she can see the workmen packing up for the
night, a chain of Christmas lights, coloured bulbs are hanging on
the scaffolding.*

    *She returns to the shelves, pulling out certain photographs.
Then she turns sharply.* NICK *is standing at the other end of one
of the aisles*

NICK: You're really doing this?

MARILYN: Don't sound like that . . . please, Nick . . . (*She glances towards the lights through the double doors.*) Is Oswald with them now?

NICK: Just gone in.

MARILYN (*softly murmuring to herself*): Oh please . . . just for once . . . let him behave himself.

INT. CAFETERIA. NIGHT.

OSWALD *is facing* ANDERSON *in the darkened cafeteria. He is standing against the wall, one arm stretched out, gently tapping the paint.* ANDERSON *is seated, staring at* OSWALD *across the table and the upturned chairs.*

ANDERSON: Can you use a personal computer?

OSWALD *continues to tap the paint.*

ANDERSON: Can you type on a computer?

OSWALD: You can do better than that.

ANDERSON: What d'you mean?

OSWALD: You can do much better than that – as a question. 'Can you type – on a computer?' – it's so banal, it's not going to tell you anything useful . . .

ANDERSON: So what should I be asking you?

OSWALD: I'd ask *you* . . . what did a freckled-faced kid in Emporia want to do when he grew up? . . . What were his dreams? . . .

ANDERSON (*deadpan*): I wanted to run a business school . . . (*Watching* OSWALD *very carefully.*) No, actually, I wanted to be Paul Newman.

OSWALD: Did you *adore* your mother?

ANDERSON: Of course . . . yes.

OSWALD: Absolutely adore her? – by which I mean, if she left you just to go down the street, down Limone Avenue, just for a few minutes . . . to post a letter say – did you feel absolutely bereft?

46

ANDERSON: Well, it depends what age we're talking about here?

OSWALD: Well, say . . . twenty-five! (*He turns.*) What sort of question is that – depends what age? . . .

VERONICA *enters.*

VERONICA: I was just wondering . . . if everything . . . if everything was . . . if you needed . . .

ANDERSON: No . . . we're just fine. (*Realising he has to remain calm.*) Now, Mr Bates . . . can we resume? –

OSWALD: Where did she come from? Your mother?

ANDERSON: Well, her family were from Ireland, first generation from around Skibbereen . . . the Kennys. (*Calm smile.*) I see you'd much prefer to interview me . . .

OSWALD: No, I don't think so – I'm fairly sure I know enough already.

ANDERSON: Mr Bates – do you really want a job here? . . . Staying on with us?

OSWALD: You doubt it?

ANDERSON: A little, yes.

OSWALD: What gave you that idea?! Sure I want a job with you . . . anything you have . . . Addressing envelopes . . . unwrapping the junk mail . . . then putting the junk mail in the bin . . . then taking the bin down to the rest of the rubbish – or garbage as you would say. (*He turns. Warm smile.*) I'm game for anything.

GARNETT *appears, standing at the back.* ANDERSON *and him exchange looks.*

GARNETT (*ushering* VERONICA): Excuse me . . . we just need a moment.

VERONICA (*glances at* OSWALD, *reluctant to leave*): Oh, I see . . .

VERONICA *exits.*

GARNETT *remains standing at the back.*

ANDERSON *leans forward towards* OSWALD *to bring*

things to a head.

ANDERSON: Can we start being serious now, Mr Bates? –

OSWALD: I *am* being serious.

ANDERSON: No you're not, you're just needling away.

OSWALD: I'm dead serious. Of course I am. After all – who
    else is going to employ a jerk like me? At my age?

ANDERSON: Apart from anything else you're not answering
    any of my questions.

OSWALD: Really? I thought I was. I'll try harder.

ANDERSON: Good – so can you clear up just one thing for
    me . . . why did you reply to all our letters, but not tell
    Ms Truman about them?

OSWALD: There were no letters . . .

ANDERSON: That's complete bullshit and you know it.

OSWALD: I don't know if you want me to say it in a different
    voice . . . maybe that would make you believe me more
    . . . Like this perhaps . . . ? (*He does it in ancient, shaking
    voice.*) There were . . . no . . . letters!!
    He looks across at ANDERSON*'s face.*

OSWALD: Is the man lying? . . . Or is he totally insane?
    Close-up of ANDERSON.

OSWALD: Or is he just a complete arsehole who can't stop
    farting around?
    He suddenly slops down in a chair.

OSWALD: But sometimes people who break the rules . . .
    however irritating . . .
    He flicks one of his shoes off, scratches a foot.

OSWALD: Sometimes, they can do things other people can't.

ANDERSON: Like what exactly?

OSWALD: Like what? . . . Like answering the question – can
    you photograph a lie?
    He looking at both of them.

OSWALD: Lying is interesting, isn't it?!
    You often think people are lying, but can that moment
    be frozen, caught there in a photograph? . . .

Not like on television programmes . . . like Nixon lying, where it's the whole general impression . . .

But instead the very moment the lie comes out . . . can a mute, still image catch that for ever? . . . As the lie escapes out of the person?

GARNETT: If we'd photographed you just now would we have snapped somebody lying?

OSWALD (*great surprise*): I'm not lying – *you're* the people lying.

ANDERSON: We are?

OSWALD: Sure . . . you're doing this ridiculous charade right now – so we'll go quietly. You're just computing when you can politely bring it to an end.

His piercing, intelligent eyes staring back at them.

OSWALD: You're doing this so there's no chance of me burning down the building, or something like that.

ANDERSON'*s eyes flick.*

OSWALD: Because natural justice will have been seen to be done –

He leaps up.

OSWALD: I mean the idea of people arriving at the American Business School of the Twenty-First Century – and the door opens . . . and who is this greeting them . . . ?

Mr Oswald Bates!

It's bloody ludicrous, isn't it! (*Dangerous grin.*) Just the image you want to put in your brochure, isn't it?! (*Smiles.*) So thank you for the interview – but I think I'd prefer to burn down the building . . .

INT. PHOTOGRAPHIC LIBRARY. NIGHT.
We cut to MARILYN *standing surrounded by neat piles that she has collected. She is staring down the length of one of the aisles behind her. She turns her head, and then starts moving towards us.*

INT. CAFETERIA. NIGHT.
We cut to the cafeteria where VERONICA, NICK *and* SPIG *are sitting obediently being addressed by* ANDERSON. GARNETT *is standing by the door.* OSWALD *is sitting a little apart.*

ANDERSON: – so we thank you for your time . . . and we just have to review how our recruitment is going for our London office . . . how many places we've got –
We see this moment from MARILYN*'s POV as she approaches across the cafeteria.*

MARILYN: I'm not doing it. The deal is off.
ANDERSON *turns surprised. Before he can speak,* MARILYN *continues, her tone powerfully controlled.*

MARILYN: I don't care how many other collections have got what we've got . . . I don't care how ridiculous and dusty and uncomputerised we are. *And* I don't care that we've got no alternative . . .
She stares at them all.

MARILYN: I've been responsible all day, sensible, grown up . . . strong . . . and it's got me absolutely nowhere!
They are all watching her. She is looking straight at ANDERSON.

MARILYN: I implore you. It's as simple as that. . . . I've got no pride about this . . . I just implore you to give me more time . . . To see if this huge, clumsy collection can somehow be found a home . . . I beg you. I don't care how embarrassing that seems . . . I BEG YOU.

INT. MARILYN'S ROOM. NIGHT.
ANDERSON*'s tone very measured, brooking no argument.*

ANDERSON: If we were to give you one more week . . .
MARILYN: Give me a week . . . Yes!
ANDERSON: If I give you a week, and it will need very

50

careful handling with the contractors, so they are fully employed on the rest of the site – I will *not* allow this to put us behind schedule . . .

MARILYN *(quiet)*: Of course . . .

ANDERSON: If I give you a week, you have to understand there's absolutely no chance of any extension beyond that. You won't be able to ask for any more. In any circumstances.

MARILYN: No, no, OK . . . I realise.

ANDERSON *(very forceful)*: I *mean* it, Marilyn.

MARILYN: Yes . . .

ANDERSON: You really think you could find somebody to house the *whole* collection in that time . . .

MARILYN *(slight smile)*: It will be a challenge, certainly.

ANDERSON: It's Christmas . . . things move so slowly in this country at the best of times!

MARILYN: I just have to try, don't I?! *(She smiles.)* It wouldn't be interesting if it was too easy . . .

INT. MAIN COLLECTION, VERONICA'S AREA. NIGHT.
(PASSAGE WITH FAX MACHINE)
SPIG *is standing staring at fax machine as it disgorges* OSWALD*'s letters.*

NICK *is standing watching the faxes come out too.*

SPIG: These are all the letters the Americans sent us.

NICK: And Mr Bates's replies . . .

SPIG *staring closer, lifting one of the fax pages up.*

SPIG: He *did* reply . . . Yes . . .

INT. MARILYN'S OFFICE. NIGHT.
We cut back to ANDERSON *staring at* MARILYN.

ANDERSON: There's one very big condition.

MARILYN (*sharp*): Which is?

ANDERSON: Mr Oswald Bates leaves these premises immediately – he has to be out of here tonight.

MARILYN *is immediately worried by this.*

MARILYN: I know Oswald seems eccentric and perverse – but he's . . . he's very gifted –

ANDERSON: Don't tell me I don't understand him! The guy's a fruitcake. How you could have ever let him handle the *business* side here I will never know! (*He raises his hand.*) And I don't want to hear now . . .

MARILYN: No – you're wrong about him.

You saw how he can find the most extraordinary things . . .

ANDERSON: I've never met anybody who's got up my nose more.

MARILYN: It's the shock of the situation that's made him behave like that.

ANDERSON: He is fired, and there is no argument.

MARILYN: If you fire him . . . it may not be easy to get people to employ him.

ANDERSON: I can't help that. This is non-negotiable. (*Their eyes meet.*) You understand, Marilyn?

MARILYN (*trying to think quickly*): It's just . . . it mightn't be the wisest move . . . it could have unpredictable consequences . . . even in such a short time.

ANDERSON (*firmly*): No – I don't believe his threats for a moment. (*Their eyes meet.*) This is what is going to happen, Marilyn.

And *you* will tell him.

MARILYN (*startled*): *I* will tell him?!

ANDERSON: Yes – you're the only one who can handle him.

MARILYN's *shocked face.*

ANDERSON: Give him any excuse you want – just get rid of him. He doesn't come back to this building ever again.

(*He looks at her.*) Is that clear?

MARILYN: Right . . .

INT. OSWALD'S ROOM. DAY.
Close-up of OSWALD *in his cardigan.*

OSWALD *gives a warm grin, remembering. Then he looks straight at us.*

OSWALD: That's what they think . . .

Credits.

SHOOTING THE PAST

Play Two

INT. GROUND FLOOR. NIGHT.

MARILYN *is staring towards us in the half-light.*
  We move in on her face.

MARILYN (*voice-over*): I've got to tell him . . . I *have* to, tell
  him.
  SPIG *and* NICK *are watching her from a little distance
  away.* MARILYN *turns to them.*

MARILYN: I've got to sack somebody I've worked with for
  twenty-three years.
  *We then move through the collection at night, past some
  pictures staring out at us, looking startling, towards a single
  lighted office.*
    There we find OSWALD *sitting by himself, surrounded
  by a clutter of boxes, papers, letters and invoices spread all
  over the place. He is looking at some weird pictures of street
  scenes of the 1930s, haunted, gaunt women staring back at
  us, like faces out of Munch.*
    There is a knock at the door. OSWALD *hardly looks up
  from the pictures as* MARILYN *comes in.*

OSWALD: They've all gone at last, have they?

MARILYN: Yes – for the moment.
  MARILYN *looks around* OSWALD's *office. There are some
  new, weird graphics scrawled on a piece of paper pinned up,
  and maps that have been covered in squiggly lines.*

OSWALD: And the world's returned to normal . . . ?

MARILYN: Not quite . . .

OSWALD (*indicating pictures*): I'm not sure you've ever seen
  these? (*We stare at the faces in the photos.*) I'm trying to
  find a sort of ghost story for the Americans . . . the story
  of these women . . . They'll be startled at the sight of
  such terrible poverty – and how comparatively recent it
  was . . . (*He looks up at* MARILYN.) You see, we stood
  our ground . . . And here we are!

MARILYN: Oswald . . . (*She hesitates.*) I got a week out of

them, to see if I can find a home for the entire
collection –

OSWALD: Terrific! We'll give it a crack – a race against time.
(*He grins.*) Could be exciting –

MARILYN: But there is a *condition* . . . (*She looks at*
OSWALD *for a second.*) They want you to leave the
building and not come back.

OSWALD *doesn't look up.*

OSWALD: Is that what they said?

MARILYN: Yes.

OSWALD (*breezily*): You didn't agree to this of course?!

MARILYN: Yes, Oswald – I had to.

OSWALD (*stunned*): You agreed to me being banished!! –

MARILYN: Oh, come on – that's being ridiculously
overdramatic – banished! It's only a week – either it's all
over then, or we'll have a new owner – and they'll rehire
you –

OSWALD: But you need *my* help to find a new owner –

MARILYN: Yes, of course. I'll be in contact all the time, in
fact you can be out and about for me –

OSWALD: But *locked* out.

MARILYN: Yes . . .

OSWALD: May I ask why?

MARILYN: Well, why do you think, Oswald?

OSWALD *stares at her.*

OSWALD: Tell me.

MARILYN (*impatient*): Because you got up their nose . . . I
did warn you . . . but you took no notice . . .

OSWALD: Up their nostrils – great! I'm glad I did. It would
have all worked splendidly if you hadn't done what they
wanted.

MARILYN: Well, you know I don't agree with that.

OSWALD: So – I mustn't set foot in this place again?

MARILYN: No, you mustn't. (*More gently.*) It'll be OK,
Oswald . . . Do you understand?

OSWALD: Couldn't be clearer!

INT. OSWALD'S ROOM. DAY.
We cut to OSWALD *staring straight at us, dressed in his cardigan.*

OSWALD: Attack – that is my advice when put in this
    situation . . . Full frontal attack – do the one thing they
    least want you to do.

INT. THE HALL. GROUND FLOOR. DAY.
Down the passages, which are bright with morning sun, comes the sound of OSWALD *humming away blithely. A moment later, he appears striding towards us as if nothing has happened. He is dressed in a clean and rather smart suit.*

INT. CAFETERIA. DAY.
GARNETT *is sitting in the cafeteria on his mobile phone.*
MARILYN, SPIG, VERONICA *and* NICK *are in a group drinking coffee at a far table.*
    They all look up, truly startled to see OSWALD.

OSWALD: Morning, everyone . . . Am I a little late? (*Moves
    over to cafeteria.*) Orange juice, Molly . . . just orange
    please, no big fry-up for me this morning. It's a new
    world, so I'm on a new diet. (*He takes orange juice.*) So
    . . . to work!
    They watch him go, GARNETT *looks across at* MARILYN.
MARILYN: I know . . . don't worry . . .

INT. OSWALD'S OFFICE. DAY.

MARILYN *comes straight through the door at speed.* OSWALD *nonchalantly sitting, surrounded by mounds of paper on his desk.*

MARILYN (*furious*): What are you doing here?

OSWALD: I considered their request carefully . . . and rejected it.

MARILYN: Oswald – you will leave here *immediately*. You are putting the whole thing at risk – quite apart from making me look idiotic. I gave them my categoric assurance you would be off the premises –
OSWALD *suddenly turns.*

OSWALD: Let me tell you something, Marilyn – you think this is childish and irresponsible, OK! – But the simple truth is . . . you won't manage it without my *help*.

MARILYN: I'm not arguing about that –

OSWALD: You will not manage it – because you don't have the first idea about what is going on out there.

MARILYN (*seething*): We'll see about that . . . But I told you, you can help me from outside –

OSWALD: If you ask me to leave – you won't get that help. I *promise* you – you won't be able to reach me on the phone, you won't get me at my house . . . You will never get help from me.

MARILYN: That's ridiculous – we're only talking about a week here!

OSWALD: Things are never simple. It would be *very* simple for me to say fine . . . I'll be a good boy, I'll sit this one out – wait patiently for you to ring to tell me if you've succeeded or not. (*He stares straight at her.*) But you *know* if I go home now – I'll never get rehired. *Anywhere.* You *know* that!

MARILYN: I don't know that – I don't know any such thing.

OSWALD: Don't lie to me, Marilyn. You think I've suddenly become an imbecile?!

MARILYN: Well, since we're talking about lying . . . I've seen all the letters, Oswald . . . The ones you said didn't exist . . . ! *Why* didn't you tell me about them . . . ?

OSWALD *staring at her for a moment.*

OSWALD: The extraordinary thing about me – shall I tell you what the extraordinary thing about me is?! . . .

MARILYN (*exasperated, half under her breath*): You haven't answered the question . . .

OSWALD: Despite what I look like . . . despite being a shaggy irritating prat . . . *I* know how the world works –

OSWALD *stares at her, as if this is enough explanation.*

OSWALD: OK? (*Waiting for her reaction.*) OK?!

MARILYN *watches him. She decides to humour him.*

MARILYN: If you say so . . .

OSWALD: Yes . . . And I'm also saying – and I don't care how over the top it sounds, you will always regret it, *always* if you ask me to leave.

MARILYN: Oswald . . . I can't believe you're making this hysterical fuss about seven days.

OSWALD: Well, I am.

MARILYN: Well, *I'm* asking you to leave.

OSWALD: Fine . . . that's the worst decision you've ever made . . . but absolutely fine . . . I've gone . . . (*Shuffling papers on his desk.*) I've left. (*He looks up at her with real intensity.*) Marilyn – you have no idea what a hash you're going to make of this. And what harm you're going to do yourself . . .

INT. OSWALD'S ROOM. DAY.
We cut to OSWALD *in his cardigan staring straight at us.*

OSWALD: Why am I making such a terrible scene . . . ? That'll soon become clear . . .

Now watch this . . . – I don't flounce out . . . *never ever* flounce out . . .

If they fire you, no stomping about . . . 'You can't treat people like this et cetera, et cetera . . .' Only makes them think they're right to get rid of you.

No begging for good references either . . . No clutching at faint straws – 'We may be rehiring people in the future.' Just say bollocks to that.

And absolutely no dignified silences . . . dignified silences are a complete and utter waste of time.

No, what you have to do is leave a lingering taste – a lingering feeling of doubt . . .

INT. MARILYN'S STUDY. DAY.
We cut to GARNETT *working on his laptop in* MARILYN*'s office.* OSWALD *appears round the door.*

OSWALD: Busy? . . . Good.
He comes into the study and plonks himself down in a chair directly opposite GARNETT.
OSWALD: Just came in to check how you're doing.
GARNETT (*sharp disbelief*): How *I'm* doing?
OSWALD: Been left here to keep an eye on these nutty characters . . . ? While your boss is off doing more important things?
GARNETT (*icy*): You could be right.
OSWALD (*leaning forward, indicating laptop*): I'm very similar to that machine, you know –
GARNETT: You are?
OSWALD: Yes. (*He smiles.*) Yes, I think that's true . . . It would be very interesting for me to take it on, my memory against its . . . I'm very good at fuzzy logic . . . making connections . . . I'll always *beat* it at fuzzy logic, and of course my database doesn't need constantly

updating – it does that automatically.

He stares at GARNETT, *who is shifting in his seat very uneasily.*

OSWALD: Clearly I'm not as easy to carry around though. (*He grins.*) But I'm working on that . . .

INT. OSWALD'S ROOM. DAY.

OSWALD: So – Marilyn starts.

I don't think she believed a single word I said.

First, she tries all the obvious people – our clients – the people we do the most regular business with, television companies, universities, documentary film-makers, newspapers, other collections –

He smiles.

OSWALD: Could she *even* get them on the phone?! . . .

INT. MARILYN'S OFFICE. LATE AFTERNOON.

Cut to MARILYN *on the phone,* NICK, SPIG *and* VERONICA *watching.* GARNETT *standing at door.*

FEMALE VOICE: He's in a meeting –

MARILYN: I wonder if you could just let him know who's calling. It's Marilyn Truman.

FEMALE VOICE: Yes . . . I'll tell him when he comes out of the meeting.

MARILYN: I wonder if you could just let him know, that I'm on the phone, because it's quite important –

FEMALE VOICE: He's just gone into the meeting . . . I'll give him the message . . . he'll get back to you.

MARILYN: Have you any idea how long he'll be in his meeting?

FEMALE VOICE (*impatient*): He's just just gone in – and oh

I've just looked, and he's got another meeting
immediately after that . . . So maybe at the end of the
day, before he goes to the airport . . . What was your
name again? Margaret what?

INT. OSWALD'S ROOM. DAY.

OSWALD: And when she *does* get somebody on the
phone . . . !

INT. PHOTOGRAPHIC LIBRARY. EVENING.
MARILYN *sitting bolt upright on the phone. Now only* SPIG
and NICK *are watching.*

MALE VOICE: I'm sorry, it's really not for us, not a practical
proposition . . . We've just acquired another 30,000
pictures – what could we do with another ten million?!
The markets flooded at the moment . . . everybody's
been selling.
MARILYN: But this collection is unique.
MALE VOICE: Oh come on, every collection is unique,
Marilyn! Best to get somebody in to cream off the top
. . . Cream your best pictures – you do still have them,
don't you? . . . ? The Man Ray and the rest? –
We cut back to OSWALD.

INT. OSWALD'S ROOM. DAY.

OSWALD: And the terrible thought hits her – she doesn't
know! She doesn't *know* if our American friends are
holding on to those pictures or not – or whether they're
for sale with everything else.

She forgot to make that a condition of her deal! –
And without those pictures she doesn't have a
chance . . .

INT. PHOTOGRAPHIC LIBRARY. EVENING.
Shot of MARILYN*'s face, tense.*

MALE VOICE: Hello – you haven't let them go, have
    you . . . ?
OSWALD (*voice-over*): At least I have taught her one good
    thing . . . to lie . . . when there's nowhere else to go . . .
    And to lie well . . .
MARILYN: No, we've still got those – absolutely! They are
    our crown jewels, after all. We can do a very good price
    – which would include everything.
MALE VOICE: Listen, Marilyn, you are never, quite simply
    never going to get anybody to take that whole sprawling
    collection – nothing works like that any more. Just save
    yourself heartache, and strip it out.

INT. OSWALD'S ROOM. DAY.
OSWALD *scratching under his arms, in his cardigan. The phone
is ringing.*

OSWALD: Take no notice of that . . . that might be her now
    . . . she's been ringing me all the time . . .
    The phone stops ringing.
OSWALD: Because she's on her own now.

INT. OSWALD'S COLLECTION AREA. EVENING.
The atmosphere is filled with smoke, the first time we have seen
MARILYN *smoking. Now only* SPIG *is watching her, sitting in*

65

the far corner. In front of MARILYN *is a long list with names crossed off.*

FEMALE VOICE: I'm sorry, I've been giving him the
    messages . . . I'm fairly sure he did try and call you –
MARILYN (*very sharp*): No he didn't . . . is he there now?
FEMALE VOICE (*slight pause*): He's in a meeting . . .
MARILYN: Can you just see – can you tell him it's me on the
    line . . . and that it's urgent. (*Suddenly.*) In fact, tell him
    I'll hold – until he's out of the meeting.
FEMALE VOICE: Just hang on a moment . . .
    There is a pause, MARILYN *stares at the clock on the wall
    opposite.*
FEMALE VOICE: I'm afraid he's not in the building.
MARILYN: You just said he was –
FEMALE VOICE: He's in a meeting – out of the building.
MARILYN: That's rubbish – can you tell him I will hold.
FEMALE VOICE: When he comes back he will call you. It is
    Christmas, you know.
MARILYN (*into phone*): I know it's bloody Christmas!
    She rings off, she looks up at SPIG.
MARILYN: Don't look at me like that – I *know* it's not the
    greatest idea to start shouting . . .
SPIG (*in a cloud of smoke*): No luck then?
MARILYN: You can say that again!
    MARILYN *suddenly moving, furiously, staring at the clock.*
    SPIG *blows smoke.*
SPIG: Can I suggest something?
MARILYN: Naturally –
SPIG: Don't sound so keen!
    MARILYN *looks across at the young girl, who is sitting in
    her haze of smoke, with her strong London accent, the
    contrast between them is striking.*
MARILYN: I'll listen to anything, Spig.
    SPIG *blows smoke.*

SPIG: Celebrity . . .

MARILYN: What d' you mean?

SPIG: Fame . . . Celebrity.

MARILYN: I know what celebrity means.

SPIG: You have to have a bit of celebrity around somewhere
. . . Nothing much happens any more without it.

MARILYN: So what's the idea – we get a famous actor in
here to ring around for us?

SPIG (*not offended*): No – of course I didn't mean something
as dumb as that.

SPIG has a pile of pictures on her lap.

SPIG: I took the liberty . . . of collecting these . . . and I just
want you to look at them for a moment . . . without asking
me anything . . . let them come at you . . . don't say a single
thing . . . just experience them.

*She lifts the pictures, a series of striking portraits of famous
people, from obvious Hollywood stars like Garbo and
Bergman, caught on boats or leaping into New York taxis
. . . to singers . . . surprising politicians like Clem Attlee in a
macintosh on the beach, to Cliff Richard in swimming
trunks, to television stars . . . and sporting stars.*

*A montage of fame of the recent twentieth century that
comes at us in hypnotic profusion. They all look luscious,
caught at the height of their youth, dreamlike in their sensual
power.*

SPIG: What did you think? . . . Wasn't it great!

MARILYN (*smiles*): Yes . . . surprised you picked some of
those, Spig – most of them were from before you were
born.

SPIG: Well, I'm not completely ignorant, you know . . . I
have picked up something from being here.

MARILYN: They're not worth a lot, I'm afraid, though –
they're all available somewhere else.

SPIG: Doesn't matter – we got 'em here. And we really need
media interest –

MARILYN: Yes, that would be good of course –

SPIG: *So* – we use celebrity – we say we've got all these
famous people here, photos to die for, and what's more,
famous people *come* here.

MARILYN: But they don't.

SPIG: Film directors have come here, for movies, doing their
research.

MARILYN: Well, we had that Spanish-Italian production
about General Franco – I don't think that's going to
make the *Nine o'Clock News* somehow.

SPIG: We lie. We exaggerate. Who's going to know the
difference! We say Hollywood directors have come here
. . . Who's to tell?!

MARILYN: It's not exactly my special area, Spig, Hollywood
directors.

SPIG *moves close to* MARILYN, *sits on the corner of the desk.*

SPIG: I could coach you, Marilyn.

She blows smoke.

SPIG: If you'd listen – I could teach you . . .

INT. WINDOWLESS ROOM. NIGHT.

*We cut to the camera moving round the windowless room, now
full not just of smoke, but cans of beer, crisp packets, overflowing
ashtrays – as* SPIG *sits drinking and smoking.*

   MARILYN *is on the phone. Her clothes still look look neat, but
the tension is showing on her face. She is doodling furiously as she
listens on the phone.*

BRISK FEMALE VOICE: – well, we did a story about an old
theatre in Clapham that's going to be turned into a club
just the other week, and we don't like doing too many
heritage stories too close together, it's become a bit of a
cliché for every local TV programme . . . But you say
Hollywood film directors use your collection . . . ?

MARILYN *doesn't respond for a second, her doodles are becoming more and more elaborate.*

Hello . . . ? . . . You did say that, didn't you?

MARILYN: Yes, we have all sorts coming here, including (*Very slight pause.*) Hollywood film directors . . . yes . . .

BRISK VOICE: Like who for instance?

MARILYN *glances across* SPIG. SPIG *makes get-on-with-it hand gestures.*

MARILYN: Like Steven Spielberg . . .

BRISK VOICE (*impressed*): Spielberg? Really! . . . Did he come in person?

MARILYN: In person? . . . (*Her eyes meet* SPIG'*s.*) Yes – I believe he did, yes . . .

BRISK VOICE (*getting interested*): What was he looking for?

MARILYN: Oh, you know – he was doing his research . . . for his next movie. (*Her doodling getting more intense. She tries to change the subject.*) Of course we have a rather wonderful collection of photos of celebrities here . . . almost anybody that's been famous in the twentieth century . . . amazing pictures of London too! . . . (*As if she is remembering her lines learnt from* SPIG.) It would be a very visual item . . . for a local news programme . . .

BRISK VOICE: So do you have any anecdotes about Mr Spielberg's visit . . . That we could use?

MARILYN (*startled*): Anecdotes?

BRISK VOICE: Yes . . . did he have a favourite picture?

MARILYN (*repeating so* SPIG *can hear*): A favourite picture!? . . . Mr Spielberg?

SPIG *making signs, which* MARILYN *can't interpret.*

MARILYN: I'm just trying to remember . . .

SPIG *making more signs,* MARILYN *mouths her incomprehension at* SPIG.

BRISK VOICE: Hello? Are you still there?

MARILYN: I think his favourite . . . I think it was of his home town.

SPIG *groans in disappointment.*

BRISK VOICE (*uninterested voice*): His home town . . . that's a surprise . . . I see . . . And have you had any stars down there with you?

MARILYN: Stars – oh yes . . . (*Sharp smile.*) A little queue of them outside the door each morning when we show up. I've got another call coming in . . . excuse me . . . I've got to go.

MARILYN *rings off sharply.* SPIG *looks across at her reproachfully.*

SPIG: His home *town* . . . ?!

MARILYN: I had no idea what those signs of yours meant!

SPIG: Couldn't you have thought of something?! . . . Dinosaurs . . . spaceships . . . extraterrestrials . . . ?

MARILYN *gets up and leans against the wall, her head going back.*

MARILYN: I don't think we have many pictures of those, Spig.

SPIG (*sternly*): You could have done better.

MARILYN (*quiet*): We have over ten million pictures . . . covering most forms of human activity, nearly everything that has gone on over the last hundred years – but we're just a tiny bit light on dinosaurs and extra terrestrials . . .

INT. OSWALD. DAY.

OSWALD: Pig's dinner . . . She's making an absolute pig's dinner, as I think you'll agree . . . The odds are stacked so heavily – it's almost unseemly . . . The thing to realise about Marilyn – she was always wonderful at dealing with all the enquiries, all our clients, but she has remained very unworldly . . . Not exactly the finger on the pulse! . . .

He smiles, a self-deprecating smile.

OSWALD: So – for a good example of somebody with their finger absolutely glued to the pulse of everything . . . We now come to my bizarre little intervention . . .

He peers at us.

OSWALD: I took it upon myself to get it from the horses mouth . . .

EXT. THE BUILDING'S GARDEN. DAY.

We see OSWALD *moving along the Victorian walls of the building. Builders' skips are lying around, pieces of scaffolding.*

He sees a blue hard hat sitting on some railings and he picks it up. He doesn't put it on yet. He moves slowly on.

He approaches where there is an entrance to the building, which has a trail of building materials coming out of it.

Just by the entrance there is a metal container, like a large rusty wastebasket, with flames lapping out of it. OSWALD *stands staring at it for a moment*

The flames begin to leap higher – disconcertingly high.

OSWALD (*voice-over, as we see him staring at the flames*): So this is clearly a coincidence that I could have done without . . . You see things on building sites, and you never know if they're meant to be like that or not . . .

As the flames leap higher, seemingly out of control.

OSWALD: Given my threats to burn down the building . . . I thought it best not to say anything!

INT. PASSAGE WITH BUILDING WORKS. DAY.

We cut inside the passage, various people standing around in hard hats at the end of the passage.

ANDERSON *is among them, but without hard hat. The air is thick with builders' dust*

71

OSWALD *puts on his hard hat and approaches.*

ANDERSON *sees* OSWALD *coming towards him. He registers his anger, in a quick glance sideways, then decides to play it restrained, polite.*

ANDERSON: Mr Bates . . . Good morning . . . What brings you here?

OSWALD (*wearing his blue hard hat*): I took the liberty – of dropping by.

ANDERSON: So I can see . . . but you must forgive me if we make this brief, because as you can see I'm in the middle of things, and this is all very technical, what's going on here –

OSWALD: Yes. It can be very technical at this stage. You want to give me a quick run-down . . . because I know quite a lot about architecture . . .

ANDERSON: I'm sure you do – but we're deep into it now . . . (*He is trying very hard to remain breezy, confronted by* OSWALD's *unexpected appearance.*) And I couldn't even repeat some of the things if I tried . . .

OSWALD (*gazing at him through the builders' dust*):Why did you have me locked out?

ANDERSON: No – that's not what's going on. As you know we're closing the collection. It's not personal. (*Slowly.*) The collection has to end.

OSWALD: So I haven't been locked out? I can come back?

ANDERSON: No – the library is closing. In a week everyone will be gone.

OSWALD: I think you were very wrong to lock me out.

ANDERSON: Well, Mr Bates – though it's not personal – I have to say you didn't seem very happy, with how we were proceeding –

OSWALD: Call me Oswald.

ANDERSON: Sure . . . Oswald . . . You found our presence very difficult, and so it's best –

OSWALD: What is all this?! Difficult . . . these euphemisms
     . . . I didn't find your presence 'difficult' – I hated you
     being there. Absolutely hated it!
     All the men, in their hard hats, are staring at OSWALD.
ANDERSON: There you are then.
OSWALD: There you are what?
ANDERSON: I'm sorry?
OSWALD: You said 'there you are' . . . Like everything was
     suddenly explained. (*He stares at him.*) But it isn't.
ANDERSON (*patiently*): If you hated us being here – it's not
     surprising you found it difficult to work with us.
          Now if you'd excuse me these gentlemen are waiting.
OSWALD: No, you couldn't be more wrong –
     ANDERSON *is getting hemmed into a corner of the passage*
     by OSWALD*'s bulky presence.*
OSWALD: I hate you being here – but that only makes me
     want to prove things to you even more. That you were
     wrong to lock me out.
ANDERSON: That seems a perverse way of looking at
     things, Mr Bates.
OSWALD: I don't believe so. And I will prove it to you . . .
ANDERSON: Well, this is very much not the time to do that,
     because I am in the middle of discussions here and –
OSWALD: I only need one thing.
ANDERSON: And what is that?
OSWALD: A picture of your mother.
ANDERSON (*startled*): Excuse me . . . ?
OSWALD: Is that difficult? A photo of your mother . . . have
     you got one about your person or not?
ANDERSON: No, I don't believe I have, no.
OSWALD (*his piercing shrewd look*): You sure? I don't want to
     use any inflammatory words like lying . . . so I'll just ask
     you again. I only need to see one picture of your mother.
     (*He smiles politely.*) Have you got one to show me?
ANDERSON: And why should you want to see one?

OSWALD: I expect you've got a little two-sided number, with a picture of both parents, like people carry . . . A little double picture? Can I see it?

ANDERSON: You just want to look at it? And then you'll leave?!

OSWALD: Absolutely. One quick look.

ANDERSON: You will leave *at once*? For good?

OSWALD: Of course.

    OSWALD *smiles.*

OSWALD: Don't feel uncomfortable – nobody's watching.

    The workmen look away.

OSWALD: I just need a quick look.

ANDERSON: I don't feel uncomfortable, and I have to warn you, Mr Bates, I will have to take the necessary steps to have you forcibly removed from these premises, if you ever set foot here again.

OSWALD: Quick butchers and I'm off! Promise.

ANDERSON (*reaching into his wallet*): This is surreal . . . I have to say . . . (*He produces a small picture.*) I know you won't tell me why you need to do this – so you take one look and then you go.

    ANDERSON *keeps hold of the picture as* OSWALD *looks at it. We see a picture of a woman in her forties.*

ANDERSON: And as you can see it's just a picture of my mother.

OSWALD (*glancing at the picture*): Right . . . is she still with us?

ANDERSON: No, she died.

OSWALD: I see. I'm sorry. (*He studies the picture for a second.*) OK! – anything on the back?

ANDERSON: No, there's nothing on the back.

OSWALD: OK . . . that's fine . . . perfect. Thank you.

    OSWALD *takes off the hard hat.*

OSWALD: Do you want this? I don't think I really need it . . .

    ANDERSON *takes the hat.* OSWALD *begins to move off*

much to ANDERSON's *relief. Then* OSWALD *turns.*

OSWALD: Don't worry. I'll be in touch.

> *He moves. then stops again.*

I hope you realise Marilyn is an amazing woman . . . and a *good* woman . . . I *hope* you've worked that out?!

ANDERSON: Sure . . . she's a very impressive person . . .

OSWALD: Sounds like another euphemism to me.

> OSWALD *leaves, then he half reappears, peering round the corner.*

OSWALD: By the way – (*Glancing over his shoulder.*) – by some uncomfortable coincidence there is a bit of a fire going on here . . . A little fire raging . . . I was going to keep quiet about it, but –

> *The builders stream past him. There is a fire burning around the building materials.*

OSWALD (*smiles sweetly at* ANDERSON): Just my luck, eh?

INT. GROUND FLOOR COLLECTION. VERONICA'S DESK. DAY.
VERONICA *is on the phone,* MARILYN *is peering down at a long list – with nearly all the names crossed through. Her face is now very pale.*

> VERONICA *is in mid-conversation on the phone, her tone very genteel.*

VERONICA: . . . it *is* a little urgent . . . so if you could just knock on the bathroom door and tell him we're on the line . . . and maybe see if he wants to speak to us . . . Yes, I understand . . . there's no point in me holding on, is there? . . . You don't happen to know what stage the bath is at, do you?

No, no. Fine. No, I quite see that . . . absolutely . . . So he'll call back as soon as he's out, will he? Thank you . . .

> *She rings off and looks up at* MARILYN.

VERONICA: Sorry . . . I just couldn't get into the bathroom.

MARILYN: Good try . . .

VERONICA *looks concerned at* MARILYN'S *drawn face.*

VERONICA: You *must* eat something, you know . . . there
will be nothing of you left soon . . .

MARILYN (*smiles*): Don't exaggerate. I'm fine. When we win
– I'll gorge myself.

NICK *comes in. He stands shyly at the door.*

MARILYN: Yes, Nick, what is it?

NICK: I've got someone.

MARILYN: What does that mean – you've got someone?

NICK: I've got someone who may buy the collection!

MARILYN: You have?! . . . You're sure?

NICK: Yes.

MARILYN: The *whole* collection?

NICK: Yes.

MARILYN: Who are they?

NICK: They are a big advertising agency . . .

MARILYN: Called?

NICK: Called . . . (*He grins.*) Good question . . . (*He tries to
remember.*) Just wait a moment, no, it's coming, (*They
stare at him, as he struggles to remember.*) I've nearly got it
– Marwood Price! – (*He smiles.*) And it's for real.

INT. THE HALLWAY. THE BUILDING. EVENING.

We cut to the hallway. MARILYN *is sitting wrapped up in a big
winter coat. Next to her is* NICK. SPIG *is directly across the
hall, giving her instructions.*

VERONICA *comes running towards* MARILYN *with a mug
of coffee, trying to hurry, but also trying not to spill it.*

VERONICA: I put in some brandy . . . d'you think that's all
right? . . . because you have an empty stomach . . . not
going to make you woozy . . . ?

MARILYN: It'll be terrific . . . thank you.

VERONICA: It's as strong as I could make it.

SPIG: So Nick will correct me if I'm wrong, but this is quite a new outfit, Marwood Price, very successful, very cool.

MARILYN: Cool . . .

NICK: Yes, they're . . . (*He stops.*)

SPIG (*impatient*): Yes, Nick, spit it out, come on!

NICK: They like to feel they're cool Brits . . . you know . . . fitting in with the whole new mood . . . They feel *they* really created the buzz –

MARILYN: So why on earth would they want us? You're sure you didn't misunderstand, Nick?

NICK: No way, no. They're very keen. Just have to persuade Mr Big.

MARILYN: Who is their Mr Big?

NICK: He's got an funny name . . . no, I'm allowed not to get right . . . it's very odd – Spittock or something like that.

MARILYN: Spittock!? – that can't be right.

SPIG: Don't worry, we'll make sure we've got it once we're there. Now, Marilyn – the only important thing is . . .

MARILYN (*smiles sipping her coffee*): There's only *one* important thing?

SPIG: Yeah – and it's to make sure we give the impression we've got other offers . . . No desperation . . . no *imploring* – that was very good before but not this time –

MARILYN: Yes, well, a woman in distress – that's all I had left that first day.

SPIG: It's the opposite now – be nice, but distant, a little chilly . . . make them feel they've got to come after *us*.

MARILYN (*slight smile*): Right.

SPIG: You'll zap them, Marilyn.

INT. FOYER OF MODERN OFFICE BUILDING. NIGHT.

MARILYN *and* SPIG, *small figures seen from a distance, standing in a glass foyer. It is deserted except for a* SECURITY GUARD. *A series of Christmas trees are dotted around the foyer with coloured lights. There is the distant sound of music and voices.*

MARILYN *is standing quietly, holding a large folder.* SPIG *approaches her, from talking at the security desk.*

SPIG: He does has a strange name – the big cheese . . . but it's not Spittock . . . it's, in fact, Styeman . . .

MARILYN: Right –

SPIG: Nick got quite close, for him!

MARILYN (*nervous laugh*): Why are they called Marwood Price then? We are in the right place?

SPIG: Yes!

SPIG *instinctively touches* MARILYN *to encourage her.*

SPIG: It'll be OK . . . you'll do great . . .

MARILYN (*sharp smile*): Well, I have to do better than I have been! This is a real chance – and what's more it's the *only* chance we've had . . .

SPIG (*hands her a mobile phone*): Here, I got Nick's for you . . . you don't have one, do you? And there's my number . . . you can ring me during it, in case you need to create a diversion . . . or ask for anything.

MARILYN *takes the phone.*

SPIG: Unless . . . ? D' you want me to be there, with you . . . ?

SPIG *looks at* MARILYN, *quite wanting her to say yes.*

MARILYN: What do you think?

SPIG: I cramp your style a bit . . . don't I? Sitting there watching you?

MARILYN: No, no, it's not that. (*She moves.*) Well, perhaps it would be best for me to talk to the boss alone – you know, head to head.

SPIG: Yeah!

SECURITY GUARD *waving at them to go up.*

SPIG: Remember, Marilyn, be chilly –

INT. PASSAGE AND OFFICE. NIGHT.

MARILYN *is escorted by a secretary down a dark passage towards light and a half-open door.* MARILYN *is clutching a large folder.*

The door is pushed open, MARILYN *is confronted by a large modern office with a Christmas tree in the corner covered with elaborate white decorations. Sitting across the room are three young people, two women and a short good-looking young man of about twenty-five.*

A door is half-open at the other end of the office, and outside we can see figures moving and the sound of a Christmas party, music and laughter.

MARILYN *cannot conceal her shock, that she is facing such young people.*

MARILYN: I've come to see Mr Styeman . . . I think that's the name,

STYEMAN: That is the name. (*Indicating himself.*) And here he is.

The twenty-five-year-old man smiles pleasantly at MARILYN. *Though he is dressed in fashionable clothes, there is something very tidy and managerial about him – old before his time.* STYEMAN *indicates for* MARILYN *to sit.*

STYEMAN: This is Laura . . . that is Simone there.

A tall man is hovering at the doorway.

STYEMAN: And Doug will be in and out – don't worry about Doug.

Some large posters, images of women's legs, cars moving across deserts, are staring back form the walls.

STYEMAN: Anything we can get you?

MARILYN: No . . . no, thank you . . .

The sound of the party and the music. MARILYN *is fighting hard not to show how out of place she feels among these young advertising executives.*

MARILYN: It's good of you to see me, I mean – (*Indicating the party.*) At the end of the day like this.

STYEMAN: Well, it sounded rather urgent to us –

MARILYN (*remembering*): No, no, that's not the case, there's no great urgency at all – we have a lot of offers . . . (*Slightly too emphatic.*) A *lot* of offers.

STYEMAN: Well, that's good. Christmas is one hell of a time to have to try and get rid of ten million pictures –

MARILYN: *I* thought that at the beginning – but it is amazing how many doors are opening . . . because of what we have to sell.

STYEMAN (*sharp grin*): So why are you here then?
The two women glance at each other, DOUG *wanders in and out, hovering in the doorway.*

MARILYN: Well, it would be stupid of me, wouldn't it, not to explore all possibilities.
We see STYEMAN *doesn't believe her.*

STYEMAN: Of course. So where are these offers coming from?

MARILYN: Well, that is confidential, just at this moment –

STYEMAN (*smiles*): You can't tell me what sort of people? Just out of curiosity, it would be good to know.

MARILYN: Well, there's another collection and a major TV company and –
She stops.

MARILYN: It's idiotic what I'm saying . . . I'm sorry . . . it insults your intelligence.
Pause.

MARILYN: Everything I've said since I came into the room is utter rubbish . . . total crap . . .
The three young people stare at her.

MARILYN: But that's *my* fault – not the collection. (*She is fiddling with the folder.*) Erase it . . . you know, what I've said so far. (*She laughs nervously.*) Can I come in again?
Somebody from the party next door pops his head round the

*door, indicating he's leaving in five minutes, and then pops
straight out again.*

MARILYN *is nervously fingering the mobile phone now.*

STYEMAN: You want to make a call?

MARILYN: No, no . . . I don't think so.

STYEMAN (*politely*): It's OK . . . you hadn't really started
. . . we've got a few minutes. Please, when you're ready,
make your pitch.

MARILYN: My pitch? . . . Yes . . . (*She hesitates.*) I'll get
down to it . . .

Their faces staring at her. DOUG *hovering in the doorway,
with his back to her.* MARILYN *suddenly takes the plunge,
decides to follow her own instincts.*

MARILYN: You're right to want to see me – even though it's
your Christmas party. Because why is this woman here?
Why is a she dragging ten million pictures around
London – so to speak – trying to find a home for them?
– That is unusual . . . and there must be a good reason
why she is so passionate. (*She begins to get into her stride.*)

And there must be a good reason too why a cool new
advertising agency should want all of them, all of these
pictures – to buy them.

STYEMAN: Yes, why *should* we want all of them?

MARILYN: I'll show you . . . I brought these along . . . just a
tiny sample of what we've got to offer. And they're
images you will have never seen before.

*She places pictures in front of them, from her big folder. She
doesn't pass them around but instead drops one after
another, every two or three seconds, in front of* STYEMAN,
like his own personal show.

*We see a series of images, very different to the ones we've
seen before. The camera peers close at them.*

*Instead of the mostly poetic photos we have seen up to
now, these are truly bizarre.*

We see hunger strikers lying in a series of glass coffins with people queuing up to watch them . . . we see a dead elephant festooned all over with tiny Union Jacks . . . we see a Sea Tractor moving across the water, tugging a hot-air balloon behind it . . . we see a bride and groom dancing on the wings of a light aircraft as it flies above mountains.

MARILYN *gives her formidable, passionate pitch as the pictures flow.*

MARILYN: There are ideas here for a hundred campaigns, it'll give you constant inspiration . . . You're in a market where it is very hard to find *new* images, things that will stop people in the street, make them suddenly look from the tops of buses. Everything seems to have been done already . . . But this will give you such an advantage over your competitors . . . whenever you're stumped for an idea, you just have to take in some of these.

STYEMAN'*S eyes flash.* DOUG *has moved back into the room, half-turned, obviously listening.*

MARILYN: Everything is images now . . . images that go straight through you leaving nothing behind – every evening we see a thousand images on the TV, but hardly any stay with us, they're almost impossible to remember an hour later. But *these* stay with you . . . photos that can haunt the memory . . . that you can look at again and again . . .

STYEMAN *glances towards* DOUG.

MARILYN: They will be an investment for you, appreciating in value. They will be a source of constant stimulation – not just providing surprising concepts for selling things, but they will also impress your clients as art objects in themselves, something far more original than just another bit of modern art. There are many pictures of immense beauty – that will afford you such pleasure . . . and bring added kudos to the firm . . .

She looks up and smiles.

MARILYN: I've *pitched* . . . I think . . .

INT. FOYER. NIGHT.

We cut down to the foyer, SPIG *is pacing tensely backwards and forwards fingering her mobile phone. Some party-goers move past her, staring at this strange young woman standing all by herself.*

INT. STYEMAN'S OFFICE. NIGHT.

We cut back to STYEMAN. *He is looking at the pictures and then up at* MARILYN.

STYEMAN: You chose *these* pictures – to appeal to an adman?

MARILYN: Yes.

STYEMAN (*quiet smile*): You chose very well . . .

DOUG *is back in the passage doing stretching movements with one arm.*

STYEMAN: That was a very eloquent presentation if you don't mind my saying so.

MARILYN (*smile*): No, I don't mind you saying so.

STYEMAN: We are used to *giving* presentations . . . and that was good.

MARILYN: Did I get anywhere, though?

STYEMAN: Yes. I think so. Yes.

Waves his hand as DOUG *moves.*

STYEMAN: Don't worry about Doug, I told you he's just making his presence felt.

You're asking how much? I know you faxed us a figure but –

MARILYN: We'll settle for 700,000.

STYEMAN: Yeah . . . (*He considers.*) I see . . .

MARILYN: That's with the Man Ray and everything . . .

Without those the price is less . . .

STYEMAN: Right. I've just got one simple question which nevertheless (*He smiles.*) . . . is of huge importance . . .

MARILYN: Yes . . . ?

STYEMAN: How much of your collection is in colour?

MARILYN *stares at him. She immediately senses she's in trouble.*

STYEMAN: A rough estimate will do . . . a ball-park figure . . . Do you have that?

MARILYN: I . . . I . . .

STYEMAN: Do you want to phone your office and check?

MARILYN: No, I know.

STYEMAN (*smiles pleasantly*): Please don't take this wrong, but we want the true figure . . .

MARILYN: It's about . . . seven per cent.

STYEMAN *whistles softly.*

STYEMAN: You're sure?

MARILYN: I'm sure.

STYEMAN: That's too bad . . . I could have gone with fifteen per cent, but not seven.

MARILYN (*very forceful*): But it doesn't diminish what I said . . . just because they're in black and white! That's daft!

STYEMAN: I know it seems banal – but that's the figure I've got in my head, fifteen per cent. It's probably garbage – like all figures . . . we *make up* the rules, just like everyone else.

He smiles at her.

STYEMAN: But that's the figure we've made up . . .

He raises his hand solemnly.

STYEMAN: But let me consider for one moment –

INT. OFFICE. NIGHT.

MARILYN *approaches* SPIG *across the foyer.*

MARILYN: It's a No.

SPIG: Oh shit . . . Really? . . . Oh fuck! You sure?

But MARILYN *is on a high.*

MARILYN: Yes . . . it's OK . . . don't worry . . . For some

reason I feel really . . . you know . . . the adrenalin . . . !
And I know what to do . . . I know exactly what to do . . .
(*Fiddling in her bag.*) Where's that number?

INT. HOTEL BEDROOM. NIGHT. INTERCUT WITH FOYER.
ANDERSON *lying on bed, his face in shadow, the sound of a television. We intercut with the foyer.* MARILYN *on a mobile phone.*

ANDERSON: Hello . . . ?
MARILYN: This is Marilyn Truman.
ANDERSON: Oh, hi.
MARILYN: Are you busy?
ANDERSON: No, not at this moment, no.
MARILYN: Good. Let's have dinner, shall we? I'll meet you
    at your hotel. At eight o'clock. Is that OK?
ANDERSON (*surprised*): Yes . . . I think I'm free . . . that'll be
    good.
MARILYN: Fine. See you then . . . I'm usually pretty
    punctual. (*She rings off.*) I'm going shopping now, Spig.
    Come and help me choose. I feel amazing . . .

INT. OSWALD'S ROOM. NIGHT.
OSWALD *staring at us in his cardigan. It is dark outside his window for the first time.*

OSWALD (*his tone very relaxed, almost humorous*): So now
    we're getting quite close to my exit from the
    proceedings. My suicide. We're beginning a bit of a
    countdown now . . .
        I want to get the maudlin bit out of the way.
        Because it is *very* important for me to try to get across
    the fact that I'm not a victim – And I really urge people

85

not to jump to snap judgements . . . 'A bit of a loser . . . so he just checked out . . .'

(*Forcefully.*) That is not what is going on here.

So to do the sentimental thing, I have some pictures here, of some people who took their own life.

We see some photos of some famous suicides. Sylvia Plath, George Sanders; and some not so famous.

OSWALD: Do we see clues? . . . About what was coming? If we stare close enough? . . .

The camera gets very close to the faces.

OSWALD: We must be really careful about generalisations, of course, but it is fair to say, they were all terribly unhappy. By and large. I think that is a pretty uncontroversial statement.

He stares straight at us.

OSWALD: But the really *vital* thing to grasp is *I'm* not terribly unhappy. No!

He scratches around his waistline.

OSWALD: Is that possible? – I can hear people saying. Can one possibly reconcile what is about to happen – with somebody not being unhappy?

He pulls himself up out of the chair.

OSWALD: Well, I have to show, in the little time that remains . . . it does make sense.

We cut to him cleaning his teeth in the bathroom mirror.

OSWALD: I'm about to go out . . . ! (*He grins.*) Big step! To get my pictures developed . . . – so people realise I've taken them. (*He smiles.*) Why I need to clean my teeth for this excursion I don't know. But there we are.

MARILYN'S OFFICE. INT. NIGHT.

We cut from OSWALD cleaning his teeth in the mirror to MARILYN making herself up in the mirror in her office. She looks stunning in a new dress, which she has just bought. NICK,

SPIG *and* VERONICA *are in the doorway watching her.*

SPIG: It's good – we made the right choice. (*To*
VERONICA.) Didn't we?
VERONICA: It's lovely.
SPIG *moves close to* MARILYN *as she does her make-up,*
staring over her shoulder into the mirror.
SPIG (*indicating make-up*): Maybe a little more . . . really
bold!
MARILYN *smiles and ignores this. The phone rings.*

EXT. PHONE BOOTH. NIGHT.
We intercut with OSWALD *in a rather seedy phone box and*
MARILYN*'s office.* OSWALD *is leaning in the phone box which*
is plastered with the usual number of sex cards for prostitutes and
massages.

OSWALD: It's me . . .
MARILYN: Oswald! At last! Why haven't you been
answering your phone? It's been ridiculous! . . . you
doing that –
OSWALD: It's not been ridiculous at all – it's been quite
restful.
Are you alone?
MARILYN: No, I'm not alone, why?
OSWALD: The others all there, are they?
MARILYN: Yes. Why? What do you want to say? I'll ask
them to leave if you like.
OSWALD: No, no – no need. (*He grins, his tone very cheerful.*)
I'm in a phone booth surrounded by Savage Swedish
Meatball massage and Sultry Spanish temptress.
MARILYN (*continuing to get ready, half listening*): Yes,
Oswald –
OSWALD: I just wanted to say I'm on to something.

MARILYN: You're on to something? What does that mean?

OSWALD: I've discovered something. You will find a full account in my flat.

MARILYN: Right. Well, maybe I'll come round tomorrow night –

OSWALD: Absolutely. That would work very well . . . Are they all still there?

MARILYN: Yes . . . (*More on him.*) Why do you keep asking that? (*She turns to the others.*) Could you just . . . for a moment . . .

The others leave.

MARILYN: They've gone now . . . What is it? Are you OK?

OSWALD: No, no, I'm fine. Couldn't be better. Make sure you give them my regards.

MARILYN: Of course . . .

OSWALD: And I just want to say –

MARILYN: Yes . . .

OSWALD: About the letters . . . I rather want to clear that up, about those famous letters that I was meant to have replied to.

MARILYN: Yes, Oswald, well, maybe we shouldn't discuss this now, I'll only get angry.

OSWALD: The fact is – it's not *quite* what it seems.

MARILYN: That's too complicated for me now. OK! You didn't tell me the truth, you lied about the letters – and that's why we're in this bloody awful mess now!

OSWALD: That's one way of putting it – but it's not necessarily the truth.

MARILYN (*exasperated*): Right! OK! I've got to go now, Oswald . . . So . . .

OSWALD (*pleasant*): Yes. Off you go . . . No problem. Got anybody to buy the collection yet?

MARILYN: No.

OSWALD: Well . . . two days left . . . anything could happen! I think I know what you're going to do. You're all dressed up, aren't you?

MARILYN *looks surprised.*

MARILYN: Yes.

OSWALD (*grins*): Just a guess! I'm sure you look terrific . . .
Go for it! I've prepared the ground . . . Go for it,
Marilyn!

OSWALD *rings off.* VERONICA *peers round the door.*

VERONICA: How was he?

MARILYN: Oh, he was just being Oswald . . .

INT. MODERN HOTEL DINING-ROOM. NIGHT.

We cut to the almost totally deserted hotel dining-room. A nasty blank room, with a little blue and red light round some plastic flowers in the distance. The faint deadly sound of Muzak.

ANDERSON *looks across at* MARILYN *as they dine surrounded by empty tables, watched by sinister waiters.* MARILYN *is in her evening dress, eating rather cautiously, conscious she hasn't had much food in the last few days.*

ANDERSON: It worked.

MARILYN: What?

ANDERSON: I can't stop looking at you.

MARILYN: Good, it was meant to work.

ANDERSON (*grins, indicating the deserted room*).The whole
town having Christmas parties – and we're here!

MARILYN (*laughing*): Clearly you booked into the wrong
hotel!

Pause. ANDERSON *looks at her.*

ANDERSON: So what do you want, Marilyn?

MARILYN: It's not what you think.

ANDERSON (*grins*): Well, that could cover a lot of things!

MARILYN: You think I want more time, don't you? Another
week.

ANDERSON (*startled*): So, do you don't want more time?!

MARILYN: No. I don't

ANDERSON: That *is* a surprise. So, what do you want then?

    MARILYN *looks straight at him.*

MARILYN: I want *you* to buy the collection.

ANDERSON: Me?!

MARILYN: Yes.

ANDERSON: The business school doesn't need the
    collection – obviously! – Otherwise we would never –

MARILYN: No. I don't mean that. I want *you* personally to
    buy it . . .

    ANDERSON *watching her.*

MARILYN: I'm sure you've got a million dollars, haven't
    you?

    ANDERSONs *eyes flicker.*

MARILYN: Someone once told me all Americans that you
    find working in England have serious money.
    (*She smiles.*) And I'm sure your trustees would let you
    buy the collection for a reasonable price.

ANDERSON: Why should I want it?

MARILYN: Because I know you're really interested in it.

ANDERSON: You're right. I've been doing my best not to
    show it – but yes, I'm fascinated by it. And also (*He
    smiles.*) . . . – despite being happily married – I also find
    you very attractive . . .

    MARILYN *smiles.*

ANDERSON: But you're making a mistake –

MARILYN: I don't think so . . . ! (*Warm laugh.*) I'm not
    trying to seduce you . . . it's not exactly my style . . .

ANDERSON: No. (*He smiles.*) You're making a more serious
    mistake than that.

MARILYN (*laughing*): More serious than that?!

ANDERSON: It's *because* I find what you're doing so
    interesting that you've got no chance with the collection.
    Not with me. No chance at all.

MARILYN: What does that mean? – I don't understand that

– sounds like something Oswald would say . . .

ANDERSON*'s tone quiet, intense.*

ANDERSON: You know I was brought up by my father, a small town businessman . . . he brought me up to *plan* everything – going to play baseball with guys on a Saturday afternoon . . . the game plan had to be laid out with him around the dining-room table the night before . . .

I think one of the great myths about where I come from . . . about American culture if you like . . . is that it is youthful, spontaneous . . . OK, some people may be like that – but there are an awful lot like me, reared right from the start to *plan*, to be in control of every situation . . . Playing old from a very young age – saying to the world, 'I'm in control . . . I've got a business plan . . . I can run this!'

This business school, the school you've shown such an interest in (MARILYN *smiles.*) is geared to a different approach – more rounded, more spontaneous – And I feel a huge passion for this, as great a passion as you do for your pictures . . .

MARILYN: There's room for both? Surely?

ANDERSON (*gently, but with real force*): Not with me – there isn't. It's precisely because I know I could be so easily diverted that you have no possibility of winning. Believe me, Marilyn, you can't win.

MARILYN (*sips her drink*): I see . . .

ANDERSON (*gently*): You want the impossible . . . you want to keep all these millions of pictures together – nobody gets the impossible any more.

INT. PHOTO PROCESSING LAB. NIGHT.

We cut to OSWALD *moving into the back room of a photo processing shop. They obviously know him here, because they greet him with familiar smiles. Asian women working there, giving him affectionate glances.*

OSWALD: Just got these – do me two sets if you could. Thank you.

He moves around in the low light of the room. All around him are the snaps of ordinary customers, hundreds of photos being sorted, processed, dried, hung up. Pictures of families, on beaches, in back gardens, in front rooms, larking around in paddling pools, getting married.

OSWALD: Other people's pictures . . . !

He stares down at them, his face half in shadow.

OSWALD: There are those who find other people's pictures totally dull . . . just can't look at them . . . But I adore them . . . Absolutely love them.

We see the everyday images, they keep flowing in front of us. OSWALD stares down at them with massive authority, his whole manner formidable and intense.

OSWALD: I just have to say one thing to make these pictures absolutely electrifying.

We see the happy smiling faces.

OSWALD: I just have to say, these people, some of these people – are about to be hit by the most terrible change. Their whole lives turned upside down.

We see more family groups.

OSWALD: And they have no idea . . .

Uncertainty beyond their wildest dreams . . .

We see birthday parties, people frolicking.

He turns to the Asian women.

OSWALD: To sound a more cheerful note I have found a mystery . . . I'm on to something . . . I've made connections . . . between things . . . In fact I really don't believe I could have done better.

The Asian women smile.

INT. MODERN HOTEL. DAY.

We cut back to MARILYN, *her coffee cup going down with a sharp movement, her eyes flick.*

ANDERSON: What's the matter?

MARILYN: I was just . . . (*She hesitates.*) Just thinking about Oswald –

ANDERSON: Don't mention him – when I start thinking of him, I begin to get really angry with you as well.

MARILYN: It's only . . . he said something odd . . . I know he likes to sound like a detective or something . . . with his little secrets . . . but he said I would *find* something in his flat – I've just remembered it. (*She turns.*) I think I might try and call him.

ANDERSON: Come on – he puts everything in an odd way, it's only because you've been out and about this week – (*Grins.*) in the real world . . . that you've started to notice.

MARILYN (*smiles relaxes*): That's true . . . you're right . . . And he did sound pretty cheerful on the phone –

INT. OSWALD'S BEDROOM. DAY.

We cut to OSWALD'*s bedroom.*

OSWALD *is lying on the top of his bed, fully clothed.*

There are several empty bottles of pills by his bed. He has just finished taking more. There's some jazz music playing in the background.

He puts the empty bottles among the cluster of others.

OSWALD: Take no chances . . . all available pills down the hatch . . .

We see some of the pictures that he's taken of himself in the room, while giving us his account. The pictures of him sitting in his chair in his cardigan fill the whole screen.

As we stare at the black and white stills they suddenly reveal a much more sombre, intense OSWALD *than the anarchic mercurial man that has been talking to us. A more haunted face.*

We move towards the bed as OSWALD *lies back. He is quietly staring at the ceiling, then he closes his eyes.*

OSWALD: I'm quite hungry, you know . . . Not sure you're really meant to feel like that at this stage . . .

We stay on him, lying there on top of his bed.

Credits.

SHOOTING THE PAST

Play Three

OPENING SEQUENCE

A photo of a young woman in a simple white Edwardian dress fills the screen.

She is seen in full figure standing next to a table overflowing with harvest festival offerings, ripe, plentiful.

We move towards her slowly, the picture taking on a different meaning as we get closer. From a distance the effect is quasi-religious, a handsome young woman in virginal white standing next to the plenty of the autumn offerings.

Only when we get really close do we see something different, a subversive, wickedly mocking look in the young woman's eyes.

And when we move from her face to the ripe fruit and crops on the table, we see sitting snugly among them an animal snare, with its metal teeth gaping open.

INT. MARILYN'S BEDROOM. NIGHT.

A darkened bedroom, phone is ringing loudly, jarringly. We don't immediately know whose bedroom it is – until an arm shoots out for the bedside light, or the phone.

MARILYN *gets the phone first.*

MARILYN: Hello . . . ? Hello . . . who is this . . . ?

For a moment there is silence, MARILYN *is still waking up, she flicks on the bedside light then she calls louder down the phone.*

MARILYN: Hello?!

There is some wheezy breathing, an intense noise, not like a dirty phone call, more like a hurt animal.

MARILYN: I don't know what the time is - but it's incredibly early, so . . . Thanks!

MARILYN *smashes down the phone. Then turns away to snuggle down again.*

And then immediately sits up again, and dials 1471. The computer voice says: 'You were called today at 4.47 hours, the caller withheld their number.'

MARILYN: Oswald! . . . (*Muttering.*) That's you, Oswald . . .
She dials his number. The phone rings.

MARILYN: Come on, come on . . .

MARILYN *is really angry but as the phone rings she begins
to get concerned. Then it clicks into an answering machine,
there is a little fanfare of music, some Tchaikovsky.*

OSWALD'S VOICE: You have reached the Bates
residence . . .

Mr Oswald Bates that is . . . not Mr Norman Bates,
for all those callers who may be familiar with the works
of Mr Alfred Hitchcock.

If you would like to leave a message for Mr Bates, and
assuming he's still around, please do so after the beeps,
and he will call you back within twenty-four hours
without fail. If of course he is still able to do so. Much
obliged. Beep.

MARILYN: Oswald? Pick up the phone, Oswald! . . .

EXT. TERRACED HOUSE. CROUCH END. NIGHT.
MARILYN *ringing the bell of* OSWALD's *small terraced house. It
is very early on a winter morning, still dark. There is one faint
light on, upstairs. Despite the early hour,* MARILYN *yells.*

MARILYN: Oswald . . . *Oswald.*

There is no response. A dog starts barking two houses away.
MARILYN *looks under the mat for a key.*

MARILYN: There was always a key . . . where have you left
it . . .

*She looks among the pile of black rubbish bags outside the
house. Then she sees at knee level, next to the door, a hook
on the wall with a key on it. A small notice says, 'Nothing to
rob – spare key.'*

INT. PASSAGE. OSWALD'S ROOM. NIGHT.

We cut to MARILYN *moving from the lighted landing to the dark of* OSWALD'S *room.*

OSWALD *is lying on the floor, his face turned away from us.*

MARILYN *rushes over to him, realising in an instant what has happened. She sees the bottles of pills by the bed, and pills scattered and squashed over the floor.* MARILYN *moves* OSWALD'S *face round towards her.*

MARILYN: Oswald . . . can you hear me . . . it's me,
Marilyn . . .

She realises he is still warm, she begins to feel his pulse, then gets the phone, yanking it towards her by the lead, so she doesn't have to move away from him. She dials 999.

VOICE: Which service?

MARILYN: Ambulance please . . . the ambulance.

ANOTHER VOICE: Hello, what –

MARILYN: I have man here – who's taken an overdose . . .
he's still alive . . . barely . . . I need an ambulance really
quick.

VOICE: Are you with the gentleman now?

MARILYN: Yes, yes, I am.

VOICE: And what is the address?

MARILYN: It is Crouch End . . . Church Lane . . . oh shit,
what's the number?! What's the number, Oswald . . .
Christ, it's sixty-something something . . . this is
ridiculous. I've just come in . . . ! sixty-seven or sixty-
eight. I've got it! –

Time Cut.

We cut to her trying the light switches. None of the lights work except the one on the landing, she sees the bulbs have been removed. She kneels again by OSWALD.

MARILYN: Come on . . . you're still there . . . you're going to
stay with me . . . because you phoned me just half an
hour ago . . . you could dial my number . . . so you can't

have fallen that deep – have you – not gone too far away? (*She lifts his head.*) Why did you take all the bulbs out – leaving just one? Typically perverse . . .

MARILYN *looks across as she tries to move him a little further towards the light. She sees for the first time the whole wall of his bedroom is covered in charts and indecipherable scrawling on large pieces of paper that he has stuck to the wall. Arrows plunge this way and that.*

And below all these charts are his tapes spread out in a neat line – and the old Dictaphone.

MARILYN: So this is what you were working on, Oswald, were you? What you were on to . . . ?

She lifts the heavy Dictaphone down so it's lying just by his face.

MARILYN: There's an ambulance coming, Oswald – it will be here any second.

She presses the button on the Dictaphone, OSWALD'*s voice immediately comes out.*

OSWALD'S VOICE: This is for Marilyn first – and then for everyone else . . . A full account of what I have found now follows –

MARILYN (*whispers*): Can you hear this? . . .

OSWALD'S VOICE: It follows *right* now.

But after OSWALD'*s voice has said this on the tape there is a hissing sound and the occasional click – the tape has nothing audible on it.*

MARILYN: Oswald, what is that for? Really?! Trying to drive me crazy to the very last –

Her face very close to his.

INT. HOSPITAL. DAY.

We see in a wide shot MARILYN *sitting by* OSWALD'*s hospital bed.* OSWALD *is unconscious, lying in the front of the shot.*

A DOCTOR'*s voice is talking quietly but emphatically as we move from* OSWALD*'s face to* MARILYN*'s.*

DOCTOR: We can't tell yet if there's been significant brain
    damage . . . we have to assume there probably has been
    some damage . . . the interruption of the blood supply to
    the brain . . . but we won't have any real idea until he
    regains consciousness . . .

    – and of course it is possible he won't regain
    consciousness for some considerable time . . . there's no
    guarantee, you understand, that he *will* regain
    consciousness.

    We are close on MARILYN *now.*

DOCTOR: Does he have family, that should be notified?
    We see the DOCTOR *for the first time as* MARILYN
    doesn't react to this.

DOCTOR (*louder*): Does he have any family?
    MARILYN *jolted into noticing him.*

MARILYN: No . . . I don't believe he has any family . . . I've
    known him all this time, and I'm not really sure, that
    must sound strange . . . But I don't *think* there's
    anybody else. Oswald's always seemed on his own, not
    in a lonely sense . . . but in a sort of unique sense . . .

DOCTOR (*beginning to move off*): So there's nobody else,
    then?

MARILYN: That's right. (*As the* DOCTOR *moves.*)
    Should I keep talking to him . . . ? I mean, aloud . . .
    even without a response . . . like you always read about
    people doing – should I be doing that?

DOCTOR: Absolutely. It can't do any harm. But I have to
    say it is rather unlikely we'll see any immediate
    improvement.

    The DOCTOR *moves off, we stay with him for a moment,*
    so we hear MARILYN *talking aloud to* OSWALD *from the*
    DOCTOR*'s POV. Her voice is angry, exasperated,*
    surprisingly tough.

MARILYN: I can't believe you've been this stupid – I really can't believe you have done this, Oswald. *Why* . . . ?!

And leaving a tape which says it will explain everything – and then it's blank, what's that *mean*? Was that deliberate?

Is this you saying Up Yours?! Come on.(*Angry.*) Tell me!

OSWALD*'s unconscious face.*

MARILYN: I still felt last night there was a chance . . . of me getting somewhere – saving the collection. And *now* I have to spend the time I've got left, vital time, talking aloud to you!

OSWALD*'s face.*

MARILYN: Oh, Jesus – Oswald help me . . .

Closer and closer on OSWALD*'s face. No response.*

MARILYN: You left me this teasing message, what can I do, specially with you like this . . . ? I've got to start thinking like you . . . (*Slight laugh.*) God forbid! I have no idea where I should start –

FLASHBACK. OSWALD'S OFFICE. STRONG EVENING LIGHT.
OSWALD *springs up, on the cut, leaping up from where he's been having a nap, on a mattress on the floor of his office. He jumps up with great energy.*

OSWALD: You caught me . . . just sneaking a little nap!
Shot of MARILYN *laughing as* OSWALD *starts straightening and doing his buttons up.*

OSWALD: What've *you* been up to anyway? . . . Are you carrying on with another visiting academic . . . ?

MARILYN (*laughing*): 'Carrying on' . . . ?!

OSWALD: Yes – carrying on . . . describes it absolutely – not too serious but definitely physical. Hope this one is better than the Norwegian . . . the walrus expert?

MARILYN (*warm laugh*): He was a lovely man . . .

OSWALD: You miss the walrus?! . . .

MARILYN *smiles.*

OSWALD: But this one is showing promise . . . ?

MARILYN (*secretive smile*): Could be . . .

We cut back to MARILYN *in the hospital looking at*
OSWALD, *a strong look. We cut back to* OSWALD, *the*
same light. He is now standing by his desk, just tucking in
the back of his shirt, staring down at the pictures on his desk.

OSWALD: You know what I think is wonderful about our
lives here? (*As he does buttons up.*) Do you know?

MARILYN: Tell me, I'd love to hear, because I'm not sure I
ever thought of it as wonderful!

OSWALD: What's wonderful is – we have a chance to dream
. . . dream from looking at these pictures . . . let the mind
float – make connections between things, daydreams,
nightdreams . . . We have space, time . . . no pressure
. . . the most valuable things on earth . . .

We cut back to MARILYN.

INT. HOSPITAL. DAY.

MARILYN: Thanks, Oswald! . . . We could still be doing that
– if you hadn't buggered everything up!

She burrows in her bag.

MARILYN: There's a major surprise – I'm not enjoying
talking like this . . . one-way conversation! – anyway the
major surprise is – that I have a mobile phone for the
first time ever . . .

She starts to dial.

MARILYN: Going to get the kids into action, since *I'm* stuck
here.

Engaged tone. She starts to dial again. A NURSE *calls*
across loudly.

NURSE: Put that away at once! . . . Mobile phones are not to
    be used here – surely you know that.

MARILYN: I'm sorry – I didn't know that . . . . (*She turns to*
    OSWALD.) Another example of me not surviving?
    Outside? Right?

    MARILYN *masks the phone with her body turning to the*
    wall, and starts phoning again.

MARILYN (*muttering to herself*): I have to break the rules –
    forgive me, everybody –

EXT. STREET. DAY.
SPIG *moving along the street going to work, swinging a large*
bag.

SPIG (*answering phone*): Marilyn?

MARILYN: Spig – I can't talk much now – something has
    happened to Oswald . . . I'm in hospital with him.

SPIG: What's happened? Is he all right?

MARILYN: He hasn't woken up yet. But hopefully he will.
    I'm trying to make him. To help him wake up . . . I want
    you to go to his house with Nick . . . the door is
    unlocked – and take anything –

SPIG: What do you mean take anything?

MARILYN: Wait a minute – listen – whatever you see that
    seems to have anything to do with this week.

SPIG (*very confused*): With this week?!

MARILYN: Yes. With him searching for something . . . and
    take it to work. *OK. Understand?*

INT. OSWALD'S HOUSE. DAY.
We cut to NICK *and* SPIG *pushing open* OSWALD'*s door. The*
room is now brightly lit by sharp winter sunlight. We can see
everything for the first time.

104

SPIG (*staring through the door*): Anything to do with this week . . . ?!

We see the full extent of OSWALD's *papers and collection of objects.*

The bath is full of old books, and a variety of old typewriters piled high. There are photos scattered around and old yellowing posters and newspapers, and a series of small bags like you might get from an upmarket confectioner, all labelled and tied up, containing various little objects.

And there is a lot of ephemera, little pieces of OSWALD's *life, old opera programmes, train timetables dating back from the sixties.*

NICK: It's weird . . . this is definitely a weird place.

SPIG: We've got to make a decision – because all of this could be to do with last week. So we've got to make a decision . . . Right or wrong. (*She moves into the room, staring at the charts on the wall.*) Everything on this side . . . (*She pulls down one of the charts.*) We take . . . everything else we leave . . .

INT. THE CAFETERIA AND PASSAGE. DAY.

MARILYN *approaching towards us down the passage that leads to the cafeteria.*

SPIG, NICK *and* VERONICA *are waiting anxiously, watching her come towards them.*

SPIG: Any news? Is he better?

VERONICA: Has he woken up yet?

MARILYN: No change. No news. (*She looks pale.*) He's still unconscious.

SPIG: He *will* get better, won't he?

MARILYN *doesn't react to this. She moves over to get a drink from the cafeteria.*

MARILYN: A cup of tea please, Molly.

MARILYN's *hands tapping along the side of the cafeteria counter, she is still full of adrenalin.*

SPIG (*insistent*): Do the doctors say he will get better?

MARILYN: Nobody knows . . . I've come back here because nobody has a clue what's going to happen . . .

SPIG *indicates the tables.*

SPIG: We put his stuff out here, we didn't know what you wanted to do with it.

The cafeteria tables are spread with the jumbled collection of objects from OSWALD's *house. The charts, posters and tapes that the kids collected.*

MARILYN *stares down at the kaleidescope of objects. She then turns abruptly, to face the others.*

MARILYN: This is our last day – (*She pauses to sip her tea.*)

VERONICA: I can't believe it! I can't believe we've not been saved by somebody yet.

MARILYN: And we can either spend a day on the phone, one last desperate ring around to see if we can raise anyone – *Or* – we can try to find what Oswald meant by all this – He told me he was on to something . . . If somehow we can work out what it was – one never knows it might do us some good.

SPIG: We should do *that*. Definitely . . .

VERONICA: What has Oswald found?

MARILYN: We don't know, Veronica . . . clearly! It's probably a joke of some kind . . . a piece of whimsy . . . It's going to mean a lot of guesswork . . . (*She looks at them.*) And the odds aren't good.

SPIG (*trying to be reassuring*): We can do it! (*Rather unconvincingly.*) I bet we can do it –

MARILYN: Right –

SPIG: But I must warn you, we just grabbed everything from one side of the room . . . if there was vital evidence on the other side – well, it ain't here . . . Just letting you know that, Marilyn –

MARILYN: I see . . . great! (*She moves towards the table.*)
Well, we've got to make some ruthless choices –
otherwise we'll still be wading through his opera
programmes at six o'clock tonight. (*She looks down at all
the objects.*) Split all this up . . . anything that seems to go
together – put it together . . .

NICK *leaps up trying to look keen, though not at all sure
what she means.*

NICK: Yeah . . . we'll do that.

MARILYN: And you, Nick – you listen to all the tapes . . . *all*
these tapes. Anything that strikes you as odd or
interesting – just call me.

She begins to move off.

MARILYN: I'm going into my study to –

Then she turns.

MARILYN: Our American friend Mr Anderson will almost
certainly turn up – to make sure that we'll be gone in the
morning. You may disagree with this – but I'm not going
to tell him about Oswald.

VERONICA (*startled*): Why? Surely they will feel sympathy if
we tell them . . . ? Maybe give us longer.

MARILYN: No. As Oswald might say, if people feel guilty
they don't want anything to do with you – It will make
us seem even more unstable . . . He'll want us out more
than ever.

SPIG: But that's going to happen anyway, isn't it!

MARILYN (*she begins to move*): While we're here, we have a
chance . . .

SPIG (*whispering to* NICK): Talk about clutching at
straws . . .

NICK: She doesn't give up!

The two young people watch MARILYN, *they are beginning
to lose faith.* MARILYN *turns in the doorway of her study,
she is looking very determined.*

MARILYN: Veronica, can you come here a minute?

INT. GROUND FLOOR COLLECTION. VERONICA'S DESK. DAY.
The two women together. VERONICA *twitching slightly, looking a little out of her depth faced by* MARILYN's *questions.*

MARILYN: You've known Oswald almost as long as I have –

VERONICA: I believe so . . . I'm sure that's right.

MARILYN: This is how I'm thinking – this is my first guess . . . It'll be about the American. Oswald probably wanted to startle the American, like he did when he found the street in Mr Anderson's home town. You think I'm right?

VERONICA: Yes . . . it could well be that . . .

MARILYN: Oswald always thought that impressed people – finding them a picture of their house from fifty years ago. So I'm thinking this is probably about the American's background, in some way . . .

VERONICA: Yes . . . it could well be that . . .

MARILYN (*sharp laugh*): Is that all you're going to say!

VERONICA *is nervous. not sure what to give* MARILYN.

VERONICA: No, I'm sure you're right.

MARILYN: Well, I'm not! (*She moves backwards and forwards.*) Veronica, can you remember – you talked to Oswald after he interrogated the Americans . . . you were there when it happened, weren't you?

VERONICA (*nervous*): I was there . . . yes – I think for a little while.

MARILYN: Now – think carefully . . . can you remember which town Mr Anderson said his family were from?

VERONICA: It was in Ireland – or was it Virginia? Ireland . . . I'm fairly sure . . .

MARILYN *flicking her hand impatiently.*

VERONICA: It was quite a well-known town, I think . . . I mean, I think it was a place I'd heard of Ski . . . Ski . . .

MARILYN *turns.*

MARILYN: Skibbereen?

VERONICA: Er . . . Yes . . . I think you're right . . . maybe
. . . yes . . . !

INT. PHOTOGRAPHIC LIBRARY. DAY.
MARILYN *is standing watching* NICK *set up a light box with
connected television so the image can be magnified and the detail
zoomed in on.* NICK *is fiddling with the machine as he finishes
setting it up.*

MARILYN: Haven't you finished?
NICK: This will help . . . I mean, to find whatever you're
looking for . . . (*He pauses for a second.*) Do you need me
to stay?
MARILYN: No, Nick.
NICK: Because . . . it's just . . . I've never seen you use this
before.
MARILYN: Nick – it's OK . . . I can manage . . . I learnt
watching Oswald.
NICK *gives her a rather disbelieving smile, and leaves her
alone.*
   MARILYN *starts slipping negatives on to the light box.
Their image appears on the television screen. All around her
there are also prints of photos of Ireland, and glass slides of
scenes from Ireland. We see pictures of an Irish town – at the
turn of the century, and also in more modern times. She
flicks through the years, jagging back and forth, she is not
spending much time on any picture – just looking for
anything that seems unusual or reminds her of something.*
MARILYN (*muttering to herself*): OK . . . so what the hell am
I looking for? Got to think like you, Oswald . . . I *can't*
think like you . . . ! (*We see images of an Edwardian
Ireland.*)
   A connection . . . something in this town, something
this family did . . . oh, for crying out loud – these are so

109

dull these pictures anyway . . . !

We see the images of ordinary folk going about their
business, either side of the First World War.

MARILYN: Is it something modern . . . ? Something
anachronistic . . . ? Something that shouldn't be there?
That was invented long before we thought it was and
kept secret? He was always good at prophecies . . . *Come*
on.

The magnified images.

MARILYN: Give me a clue . . . something!

FLASHBACK. INT. OSWALD'S STUDY. HOT SUN.
OSWALD *sitting on the edge of his desk, swinging his legs. He*
looks much younger.

OSWALD: I saw somebody on the street with a phone – a
portable phone! A big heavy thing! Soon – I bet
everybody will have them . . . much quicker than you
think . . . Builders will have them on building sites, bin
men will have them, piano tuners, secretaries, the whole
world! I bet you . . .

INT. PHOTOGRAPHIC LIBRARY. DAY.
We cut back to the magnified images that MARILYN *is looking*
at . . . and then her face, intense with concentration, staring down
at them.

MARILYN: So what happened!? The talkies were invented
here . . . ? long before *The Jazz Singer*? . . . A military
catastrophe . . . ? Something nuclear . . . ? (*Staring at the*
images of the peaceful town.) Doesn't look like it!

INT. WINDOWLESS ROOM. DAY.
We cut to NICK *listening to* OSWALD's *voice on the Dictaphone.*

OSWALD'S VOICE: Together they will form something hopefully that can be kept, published, even used by the mass media . . .

    NICK *grins at this claim, shakes his head in disbelief.*

INT. PHOTOGRAPHIC LIBRARY. DAY.
We cut back to MARILYN *staring at the pictures.*

MARILYN: Something domestic then . . . ? Something much more personal? . . . Passionate? . . .

INT. HALL FIRST FLOOR. DAY.
We cut to ANDERSON *crossing the hall looking around him, staring at the strange objects laid out on the table.*

    The cafeteria is momentarily deserted.

INT. CAFETERIA. DAY.
He moves towards the door of MARILYN's *study. He can see it is ajar.*

INT. PHOTOGRAPHIC LIBRARY. DAY.
We stay with him as he pushes open the door and sees MARILYN *across the darkened study, her face illuminated by the light box.*
MARILYN *is in mid-sentence, muttering to herself.*

MARILYN: Something sexual – more likely . . . something sexual, powerful? Something really passionate?

MARILYN *looks up sharply. She is totally preoccupied with her search, and is unembarrassed to be found talking to herself.*

MARILYN: There you are! Bit earlier than I was expecting. I'm not packing up till the end of the day –

ANDERSON: Fine. You've got till the end of today – that's what we agreed.

MARILYN: So you're holding us to that timetable, are you?

ANDERSON: Marilyn! Come on –

MARILYN: No, I know . . . just checking –

She looks down at the light box, then up at him.

MARILYN: You don't have a picture of your mother on you, do you?

ANDERSON *looks startled at being asked this again.*

MARILYN (*looking straight at him*): Do you have a photo of your mother? Or even better of your grandmother? . . .

ANDERSON: What is this?! Why this obsession with my mother? That's what Oswald asked me!

MARILYN (*excited look*): He did?! That's great!
(*Sharply.*) When did he ask you?

ANDERSON: When?

MARILYN (*impatient*): Yes – it is *important* when he asked – mid-week was it?

ANDERSON: Yes.

MARILYN: Good –

ANDERSON: He *insisted* on seeing a picture of my mother –

MARILYN: He probably thought you wouldn't be carrying a picture of your grandmother, most people don't, you're not, are you?

ANDERSON: No! –

MARILYN: So he was right, as always. (*Sharp.*)
Where's the picture of your mother?

ANDERSON (*amused at her urgency*): Here . . .

MARILYN (*she watches him take a photo out of his wallet*):
There she is . . .

112

ANDERSON: She died five years ago . . .

MARILYN (*staring at her*): I'm sorry . . .

> ANDERSON *watches* MARILYN *as she places the picture under the magnifying lens. And then passes other pictures under it trying to find a woman that looks like her.*

ANDERSON: Trying to find something out about my background?

MARILYN: You bet.

ANDERSON: So Oswald didn't get anywhere?

MARILYN: On the contrary – (*She stops.*)

ANDERSON: He did? So why don't we ring him up and ask him?

MARILYN: He's ill.

ANDERSON: Too ill to call?

MARILYN: He's not taking calls . . . (*Looking straight at him, challengingly.*) What are you doing here anyway?

ANDERSON: I came to check on your progress –

MARILYN: Really? Well, I'm making progress right now . . .

ANDERSON: Got anybody to buy the collection?

MARILYN: Some promising leads . . . which are still warm . . . could come through at any moment –

> ANDERSON *smiles at this.* MARILYN *is staring at a picture of a woman who looks fairly similar to* ANDERSON's *mother – then she decides to move on.*

ANDERSON: There is nothing there, Marilyn –

MARILYN: Nothing where?

ANDERSON: In my background . . . can tell you about my grandmother . . . there are no surprises there . . .

MARILYN: You reckon? (*As she stares at pictures.*) Tell me –

ANDERSON: She was the daughter of a local businessman in Skibbereen. They were quite affluent, in fact. She went with an aunt on a trip to the US when she was in her early twenties, to visit relatives. And there she met my grandfather at a tea dance . . .

> She was a dutiful wife by all accounts and she had just

113

the one child, my mother.

I believe she lived for my grandfather – as often happened at that time. (*Moving closer to* MARILYN *as she stares at him.*) She died when I was two years old. I have no memories of her. (*He stares down at the images.*)

There is nothing to discover . . .

MARILYN *takes no notice of this, she is scouring the faces of the women in the pictures.*

MARILYN: She must be here –

ANDERSON: Why must she be here?

MARILYN: Because I think Oswald found her . . . She's here . . . she's definitely here . . .

Suddenly she bends really close.

MARILYN: And I think I've found her . . .

We see a very handsome young woman standing at the back of a group photo of four demure-looking women in Edwardian dresses. We move in on her, there's a glinty look in her eyes.

ANDERSON (*staring carefully*): It could be . . .

MARILYN: It is.

ANDERSON: It *could* be.

MARILYN: *It's your grandmother.* Meet her as a young woman . . .

ANDERSON: OK – there's a good likeness . . . I'll give you that . . . Great you've found the picture . . . can I keep it?

MARILYN: No. Absolutely not . . . Certainly not yet!

She picks it up. Begins to move.

MARILYN: Come on, it's the beginning of the trail . . .

INT. CAFETERIA. DAY.

We cut to the camera moving over all the pieces from OSWALD'S *room, which are now separated into sections, all the charts together, all the opera programmes, all the peculiar metal objects.*

ANDERSON *is moving down the table with* MARILYN,

SPIG *and* VERONICA *watching them from across the room.*

MARILYN: Is there anything here – please look – that has something to do with your family? Anything that you recognise?

ANDERSON (*smiles at the bizarre collection*): I don't believe there is, no.

    MARILYN *looks closely at the charts, with the arrows pointing in various directions and the words scrawled on them.*

MARILYN: Any of these words make any sense to you?

ANDERSON: No . . . (*Staring at the scribbled words.*) Seems a lot of the same word . . . is it 'Gunge something' . . . ? (*He smiles.*) 'Gungerama'? . . .

    MARILYN *stares at the word beginning with G that appears all over the charts.*

MARILYN: No, it's not 'Gunge something', maybe it's Gadgetry?

ANDERSON: No, no way that's Gadgetry . . . Grenadier?

MARILYN: Or 'Gadarene' maybe? . . . Could be Gadarene . . . (*She turns.*) Does that convey anything?

ANDERSON: Gadarene . . . ?! No . . . It conveys nothing . . . (*Looking down at the word.*) Absolutely nothing.

MARILYN: Spig – could you go and see if there's anything under Gadarene in the collection.

INT. COLLECTION. DAY.

SPIG *in the collection . . . moving among the aisles, leaping up to see what the boxes on the very high shelves say.*

INT. CAFETERIA. DAY

We cut back to the cafeteria, ANDERSON *still trying to make out the word, his manner jokey.*

ANDERSON: Could be Gaderini . . . It's probably one of
   Oswald's favourite restaurants . . . !

   MARILYN *stares at him very coolly for a moment, as he
   laughs.*

MARILYN: Haven't you got to keep to your busy schedule?
   Isn't there an important meeting with architects – you
   should be at?

ANDERSON: Not today – no . . .

MARILYN (*pointed*): Then you can really be put to work,
   can't you – help solve this –

ANDERSON: I don't see what there is to solve – you find a
   picture of my grandmother as a young woman and –

MARILYN: I'll tell you what there is to solve!
      Somewhere in there – (*She stares down the aisles of the
   collection.*) – is what happened next.

   ANDERSON *follows her gaze.*

MARILYN: We just have to make the connection.

INT. COLLECTION. DAY.
We cut back to SPIG *searching. She is passing some very old
shelves – having walked past them, she stops as if she's seen
something, and moves back. Something has caught her eye among
the most battered boxes. She lifts one down, and rubs the very
dusty label. She can just make out Gadarene. She opens it. She is
greeted by bristling faces of various wild boars staring back at her,
some very large pigs, their snouts pushing out at us.*

   We cut back to the cafeteria.

INT. CAFETERIA. DAY.

ANDERSON: Wait a minute . . . 'Gadarene'? There's
   something biblical, isn't there? . . . It's just coming back
   – my Bible classes – wasn't there something about the

Gadarene Swine . . . hogs . . . they threw themselves off a cliff . . .

SPIG *is entering at this very moment holding pictures.*

MARILYN (*to* SPIG): *Yes?*

SPIG *stops, rather embarrassed.*

SPIG: It's just a load of pigs, I'm afraid.

ANDERSON *smiles.* MARILYN *takes the box, looking at the pictures.*

SPIG: A lot of porkers . . .

ANDERSON (*also looking at the pigs amused*): I really don't believe my family has ever had much to do with the Gadarene Swine!

MARILYN: Yes, well . . . there may be other boxes, of course . . .

ANDERSON: Come on, you're building a house of cards here . . . You *think* it is my grandmother . . . this word here might be 'Gadarene' – it's not going to add up to anything, Marilyn –

The phone rings. VERONICA *answers it.*

VERONICA (*voice very quiet*): Yes . . . no . . .

MARILYN (*immediately urgent*): Is it the hospital? Is it about Oswald? (*She moves towards phone.*)

VERONICA: I see . . . (*She shakes her head at* MARILYN.)
MARILYN *doesn't for a moment know what this means, whether it is bad news from the hospital.*

VERONICA (*into phone*): No – we're still open, and we can do that, yes, a full set of British Prime Ministers of the Twentieth Century . . . yes . . . Right up to the present day . . . yes, the setting doesn't matter?

ANDERSON: A hospital? Has Oswald been in an accident?
MARILYN *turns to look at him.*

INT. MARILYN'S OFFICE. DAY.
MARILYN *and* ANDERSON *facing each other.*

MARILYN: Oswald tried to kill himself.

ANDERSON (*eyes flicker*): I'm sorry, really sorry to hear that.

MARILYN: He's in a coma.

ANDERSON (*quiet*): Is there anything I can do?

MARILYN: No. I don't think so . . . That is good of you . . .
(*Slight pause.*) I was expecting –

ANDERSON: What were you expecting?

MARILYN: For you to be angry in some way . . . you know,
because . . .
She not sure how to put it.

ANDERSON: Because of what?

MARILYN: You know, maybe . . . (*She looks at him.*) Feeling
guilty about things? –

ANDERSON: I don't feel guilty. (*He looks at her, tone gentle.*)
Do *you* feel guilty?

MARILYN: Yes, a bit, because . . . (*Suddenly.*) Oswald's not
the fruitcake you think he is . . . I mean, he's not easy, I
grant you – but he's a very . . . a very modern person.

ANDERSON: Modern? You're kidding!

MARILYN: No – he is. His mind works very fast, really really
fast. He knows everything that's going on. . . . I just feel I
should have kept up with him . . . seen his darkness.

ANDERSON: I can't understand why after just being asked
to leave a week early – he should try to take his life
because of that!

MARILYN (*quiet*): I don't understand that too. Not at the
moment. We might never know. . .
She is doodling, drawing a series of Gs.

MARILYN: I also don't know if he left this puzzle
deliberately, to *test* me . . . or it was a mistake, the
incompleteness – (*She picks up photo.*) Well, you can
have the picture of your grandmother, take it. And it *is*
her.

VERONICA *comes in, having given a little polite knock.*

VERONICA: Excuse me – I just want to check – that I

118

haven't missed out any Prime Ministers of the Twentieth Century, my memory, you know, is not what it was. (*She puts the photos in front of* MARILYN.) I nearly left out Bonar Law.

MARILYN: OK, I'll look at them.

VERONICA: Very good. (*As she leaves, pointedly to* ANDERSON.) You see, we're *still* open for business.

MARILYN *begins to flick through the photos. Familiar faces, Churchill, Harold Wilson, Thatcher, Macmillan, Baldwin.*

ANDERSON *watches* MARILYN, *his tone is concerned, wanting her to listen.*

ANDERSON: You *still* can make your selection – take all the pictures you want . . . The offer is open – you know that. Save bits of the collection, Marilyn –

MARILYN *seemingly oblivious as she looks at the PMs.*

MARILYN: I don't think there's anybody missing –

Suddenly MARILYN *leans forward, shuffles the pictures abruptly, and goes back to a picture of Edward Heath. The picture is of Heath conducting an orchestra.*

ANDERSON: What's the matter?

MARILYN *stares at the picture of Edward Heath.*

ANDERSON *looks at the picture from across the desk, upside down.*

ANDERSON: I don't think I know this guy . . . (*He turns the picture towards him.*) He's the guy that hated Mrs Thatcher?

MARILYN (*completely oblivious*): I think . . .

ANDERSON: What's so significant about him? . . . (*He grins.*) You're not going to tell me I'm related to him?!

MARILYN: No . . . it's not him that's important . . . something's occurred to me. (*She looks at the musicians.*) I've just remembered . . .

MARILYN *gets up.*

MARILYN: Give me a moment – just to make sure . . .

You wait till you're called –
She moves off, then turns back to the desk. She picks up the picture of the grandmother, and pushes the photo of Heath towards ANDERSON. *Then she leaves.*

INT. COLLECTION (VERONICA'S PART). DAY.
We cut to MARILYN *in the darkened part of the collection. She lifts a box down. A beautiful glass slide of a cello . . .*

INT. MARILYN'S OFFICE. DAY.
We cut back to ANDERSON *who has moved away from the desk, staring around* MARILYN'S *world, all the things she has in her office.*
    SPIG *appears in the door.*

SPIG: She's ready for you now.

INT. BASEMENT COLLECTION. DAY.
ANDERSON *approaches down the aisles of the collection.*
    MARILYN *is waiting for him in the distance, at the end of the collection, it opens out, and there is an expanse of floor – a totally empty space. She has a series of photo boxes laid out in a line on the wooden floor. She is standing very poised, very calm, waiting for them.*

ANDERSON: OK, here I am . . . (*He reaches her.*) What you got for me?
MARILYN (*nonchalantly*): Oh, one or two little things –
ANDERSON: Just little things? OK – (*He smiles.*) I have to warn you, Marilyn, I'm very sceptical . . . you can show me any picture, absolutely anything . . . a guy with antlers on his head – and say this jerk here is your great-

120

uncle! How am I meant to know?! You have no proof about anything –

MARILYN: We'll see about that.

ANDERSON (*smiles*): *There is no proof.*

MARILYN: If you say so . . . (*She looks at him.*)

   Why do you want to distance yourself from it, before you've even heard what it is?

ANDERSON: Because you and Oswald must think – you've got some ammunition . . .

MARILYN: It's too late for ammunition, isn't it?

ANDERSON (*smiles*): Much too late . . . (*Then looking straight at her.*) So is it something unpleasant you've dug up?

MARILYN: Depends on your point of view.

ANDERSON: Marilyn! –

MARILYN: It's a great story. (*She looks at him.*) *I* think it is.

   ANDERSON'*s eyes flicker.*

MARILYN: But of course you may not have time to hear it.

ANDERSON: I don't believe a word of it – whatever it is . . . (*He grins.*) You're just guessing all the time . . . (*He sits.*) But give it to me.

MARILYN: Aren't you worried we're not packing up yet? . . . We should be getting our things together, shouldn't we, ready to leave?!

ANDERSON: Tell me what you've found, Marilyn! . . .

   MARILYN *moves towards the boxes.*

MARILYN: Are you musical?

ANDERSON: A little. Nothing special.

   I play a bit of piano . . .

MARILYN: OK . . . just wondered . . .

   She kneels on the floor. Takes first photos out of their boxes. And she lays them out on the wooden floor. Soon they will form a trail across the floor, like a line of dominoes, snaking around them.

   We see the first pictures. They fill the screen. Houses.

Stately homes, and large affluent country houses.

ANDERSON (*grins*): Great houses! . . .

MARILYN: Great houses, yes.

ANDERSON (*grins*): Are you going to tell me one of them
   belongs to me . . . ?!
   *We see pictures of grand parties, balls, big wedding
   receptions, people dancing under fairy lights in the grounds
   of great houses.*

MARILYN: This is just before the First World War, society
   wedding parties, New Year's Eve parties . . .
   *We move in on the musicians. We see various different
   groups playing from photos of the period, musicians
   accompanying the waltzing couples.*

ANDERSON: Is she dancing? Somewhere there . . . 'my
   grandmother'? (*He stares at the couples beginning to be
   fascinated.*) Is she in a terrific ball-gown being swept off
   her feet?

MARILYN: Just like now, there were musicians who
   specialised in playing at society occasions, weddings,
   balls – they would travel from great house to great
   house –
   We move through images of musicians.

   MARILYN *stops at one particular picture. A group of
   musicians standing poised against the backcloth in a studio.
   There is something different about them – almost subversive.*

MARILYN: There was one group of musicians – these –
   called the Minotaur Orchestra. There's something quite
   charismatic about them, isn't there?

ANDERSON: The Minotaur Orchestra? . . . (*He grins.*) More
   animals?

MARILYN: Your grandmother Hettie must have met them
   when they came to play at a ball she attended in
   Cork . . .
   We are moving in on ANDERSON who is looking startled.

ANDERSON: Hettie . . . how did you know she was called

122

Hettie? I never told you that.

MARILYN *moves the original picture of Hettie in her virginal group of girls in front of them.*

MARILYN: Because this Hettie . . . this innocent Hettie from Skibbereen is going to join up with another sort of Hettie . . . a Hettie we knew about already – Oswald and I.

ANDERSON *puts the virginal pictures of his grandmother next to the picture of the Minotaur Orchestra.*

ANDERSON: So she ran away with somebody from this orchestra?

MARILYN: No. She joined the orchestra. As a full member.

We see pictures of musicians playing . . . original pictures of the period flicking past us.

And then we see an image of Hettie playing the violin in an evening-dress, while somebody in a lavish ball-gown dances in the foreground.

ANDERSON: That's good . . . I like the idea – that's romantic . . . she plays at these great dances . . . mixing with aristocracy . . . a woman musician . . . that's great!

The pictures are coming thick and fast of British society at play just before the First World War. MARILYN *is moving on.*

ANDERSON: Hang on a moment . . . ! (*He is staring captivated at Hettie playing the violin.*)

MARILYN: These *now* are the pictures I was able to put together because I got the connection . . . I got the connection that Oswald made. We had this story . . . we knew where it went . . . we had never found the connection with Ireland – where Hettie came from . . . we never traced it back, until Oswald started digging into your background –

ANDERSON: So you found my grandmother playing in an orchestra –

MARILYN: Your grandmother is going to surprise you . . . (*She smiles.*) I really believe she is . . .

ANDERSON: She has already surprised me. If, of course, this
woman has anything to do with me . . .

MARILYN *moves off up the stairs out of the basement.*
ANDERSON *has to follow, if he wants to hear any more.*

INT. GROUND FLOOR. OSWALD'S OFFICE. DAY.
ANDERSON *comes into* OSWALD'*s office where* MARILYN *is
standing waiting for him holding a further instalment of pictures.
As he approaches her,* MARILYN *resumes the story. As she
speaks we see provincial towns just before the First World War.*

MARILYN: Hettie – your grandmother – travels from great
house to great house with the Minotaur Orchestra . . .
but there is *something* about this band! They start to give
little parties of their own, the nights before they play at
the big houses . . . while they stay in whatever town they
are visiting . . . Behind closed doors . . . they hold their
own wilder parties! . . .

MARILYN *puts the pictures in front of us, we see a small
room, people playing music, while others dance, scantily
clad, a lot of drink around. And on the wall a banner is
hanging . . . we move in closer and closer to the photograph
until we can read 'The Gadarene Club'.*

ANDERSON *stares at the image, being drawn more and
more into it.*

ANDERSON: That's amazing . . .

MARILYN: Yes . . . it's good, isn't it?

ANDERSON: But this is a set-up, isn't it, Marilyn?! This
funny word scrawled on bits of paper by Oswald – like a
serial killer . . . 'Gadarene' . . . And now here it is – how
convenient! And suddenly all these pictures – You're
giving me this tale – and maybe I'm getting hooked . . .
but I'm very suspicious –

It's so easy – let's find something in his background.

124

Wow! – there *is* an interesting story! – and then lo and
behold! – here are all these photos to go with it –

MARILYN: Well – wow there is a story, *yes*! And wow – you
haven't heard the half of it yet!

ANDERSON: Tell me then . . . get to the real Hettie.

MARILYN: You want it short and brutal then?

ANDERSON: Not brutal . . .

MARILYN: The Gadarene Club is not just dancing after
hours . . . They are quite adventurous these young
people . . . artistic . . . they start taking their own pictures
– what we'd call surrealistic pictures.

ANDERSON: Yeah, they're weird . . . sensual . . .
*We see pictures of Hettie like the harvest festival one in the
beginning sequence. They are disconcerting, powerful. In
some of them she is semi-nude. There are images of metal
and flesh, of a pig's head and balloons.*

*And we see Hettie with two tall men, standing next to her
. . . Although they are fully-clothed there is a strong sense of
sexual abandon . . .*

ANDERSON: She's having an affair with one of these guys?

MARILYN: No she's not. With *both* of these guys.

ANDERSON: Both? –

MARILYN: Yes – the tall one is called Neville, the really tall
one is Robert . . .

ANDERSON: How do you know she was involved with both?

MARILYN: I could say look at the picture!
But also I know because soon after they played a ball
at Hilton Castle in Derbyshire . . .
*The pictures come in a rush now . . . photos of the Peak
District, of a castle, of lonely roads, of police searching the
moors.*

ANDERSON (*his voice quiet*): And what happens there?

MARILYN: At Hilton Castle, both men suddenly vanished.

ANDERSON: Vanish! Both of them?

MARILYN: Both of them – Neville Dawson and Robert St

Barry have disappeared.

Hettie is questioned by the police – search parties are sent out . . . .there are newspaper articles . . . two men vanish off the face of the earth.

Hettie is reported as having been 'close friends' to both men – but nothing is found, not a trace of them turns up, even on the moors –

ANDERSON: An English mystery . . .

MARILYN: For the moment, yes . . . Hettie is never charged with anything and –

ANDERSON: How could she be? . . . She's not guilty of anything! . . . Clearly . . . !

MARILYN *moves off again. This time* ANDERSON *follows her urgently.*

INT. GROUND FLOOR COLLECTION. VERONICA'S DESK. DAY.
They move into the darkness of VERONICA'*s room where there are light boxes etc.* MARILYN *has some new pictures. Her tone is more urgent, the cuts of the pictures quicker. We keep seeing Hettie's face coming at us, the anarchic surrealistic pictures and poses, and her sharp glinty eyes.*

MARILYN: It was assumed the two men must have run off somewhere – to America perhaps – because they were involved in crime –

ANDERSON: That sounds very plausible to me –

MARILYN: That wasn't what happened though . . .

MARILYN *and* ANDERSON'*s eyes meet.*

MARILYN: Hettie disappears from view. Nobody in this country ever photographs her again . . .

MARILYN *watching* ANDERSON.

MARILYN: But she was still somewhere in this collection.
She glances towards the aisles of photos tapering into the distance.

MARILYN: And Oswald found her.

> MARILYN *moves off,* ANDERSON *watches her go,*
> *fascinated. He doesn't move immediately, lets her get away*
> *from him and then follows.*

INT. COLLECTION. GROUND FLOOR. DAY.
ANDERSON *finds* MARILYN *spreading the final pictures out*
on the bare wooden floor of the main collection. MARILYN *drops*
the first photograph in front of ANDERSON.

MARILYN: There . . . In Paris after the First World War . . .
ANDERSON: A new Hettie . . . yes . . .

> *We see Hettie sitting at a café, her hair different, very*
> *relaxed pose, a rather daring dress, showing her private*
> *daring in public now.*

MARILYN: Here she is – part of *your family*. Your flesh and
blood!
ANDERSON: I only have your word for that.

> *A look in* MARILYN*'s eyes.*

> *We see lots of photos of Paris in the twenties, artists,*
> *prostitutes . . . Again they come in a vivid rush. And, in*
> *among them, more surreal pictures of Hettie in a small dark*
> *sitting-room, her very pale face.*

MARILYN: She is living in a strange world . . . some of it is
semi-conventional, she works as an artist's model . . .
But again, behind closed doors, other things happen. A
weird claustrophobic world –

> *We see another picture of Hettie in a darkened room, we*
> *move across the surface of the picture slowly.*

MARILYN: A very intense world . . .
ANDERSON (*staring fascinated*): Full of sex and pictures, it
appears –
MARILYN: Lots of sex clearly, drugs . . . seances maybe . . .

> *We are still moving across the surface of the picture.*

127

MARILYN: See who's next to her?!

We see the tall figure of Neville Dawson standing behind Hettie in the shadows.

ANDERSON: There he is . . . ! (*He stares into Neville's eyes.*) No Robert?

MARILYN: No Robert . . . (*She stares at him.*) Definitely no Robert . . .

ANDERSON: Why do you say that? . . . *Definitely* no Robert . . . (*Very involved.*) You've no right to say that . . . cast suspicion on her . . . he could be anywhere . . .

MARILYN: He was.

ANDERSON: You're not implying that Hettie was involved with murder? That this woman was a murderer?

MARILYN *stares at him. She smiles slightly.*

ANDERSON (*really involved*): No way is this woman a murderer? Who says Robert wasn't there anyway?!

He could be there – and nobody took a photograph! *He* could have taken all these photographs himself!

MARILYN (*very final tone*): He *was* there once.

Close-up of ANDERSON.

MARILYN: When the house was demolished – the house where Hettie had her apartment . . . When it was demolished . . . human remains were found under the floorboards.

ANDERSON: You're making this up! –

MARILYN: Under the floorboards of that very apartment.

ANDERSON: Some of this may be true . . . but that is obviously made up!

Pause.

MARILYN: You don't believe me . . . OK . . . (*She calls.*) Spig . . . Spig . . .

SPIG *walking towards* ANDERSON *with a box. She splashes French newspaper cuttings of a body in an apartment down in front of him.*

SPIG (*innocently*): Do you read French . . . ?

ANDERSON: I read French . . .

Time Cut.
We travel the trail through the pictures of Hettie's life.
ANDERSON *follows the trail, absolutely captivated . . . though*
still only half believing. We see Hettie in her virginal white, then
in the music parties, then in the surrealistic pictures.

MARILYN (*voice over the pictures*): Oswald found these all
    himself . . . he made the connections.
       He found her again and again . . . in the music parties
    before the First World War . . . In Paris after the war . . .
    he found the apartment . . . he sent for the cuttings . . .
    He followed the Trail –
ANDERSON (*suddenly*): But it all could be bullshit.
MARILYN: Oh yes . . . ?

    ANDERSON *looks across at* MARILYN. *He is standing the*
    other side of all the pictures.
MARILYN (*challengingly*): Want to know if there's another
    picture?
    Silence. ANDERSON *watching her.*
MARILYN: Want to?

    MARILYN *is holding something.*
ANDERSON: What is that – what have you got there,
    Marilyn?
    She walks up to him and drops the picture down on the
    windowsill. At first we don't see what's in the photograph.
       ANDERSON, *a very startled look.*
ANDERSON (*soft whistle*): Jesus . . . !
    We then move on to the picture.
       First we see Hettie sitting at a table drinking, now much
    older, her hair wild, looking dishevelled, and rather poor and
    mad . . . We then move over to who she's looking at.
       ANDERSON'*s mother is sitting next to her, drinking*
    wine, in the small room, with candles flickering. On her lap

129

is a baby, a year-old boy staring up at the rather mad
Hettie.

MARILYN (*quietly*): Your meeting with Hettie . . .

ANDERSON *is absolutely transfixed.*

*The camera moves back across the picture. Hettie, his
mother, and the one-year-old* ANDERSON *on his mother's
knee.*

*And then the camera moves closer, past them on to the
wall of the room, where a rather soiled banner is pinned up –
the Gadarene Club.*

INT. MARILYN'S OFFICE. DAY.

(DOOR OPEN TO THE COLLECTION.)

We cut to ANDERSON *sitting drinking tea in* MARILYN'S
office.

*Despite sitting in a deep armchair, with teacup, he is full of
adrenalin, his mind racing.*

MARILYN *is also drinking tea, leaning against her desk.* SPIG
and NICK *watching from the door,* VERONICA *hovering in the
passage.*

MARILYN: Is that better?

SPIG (*grins*): Or do we need to get you something stronger?

ANDERSON: No – tea to calm me down . . . ! No, that's
fine . . .

MARILYN *indicates the others should leave.*

MARILYN: I don't think he needs your first-aid, Spig . . .

The others leave.

ANDERSON *smiles, his whole manner is charged with
excitement.*

ANDERSON: I don't think it *is* working somehow . . . the tea.

He begins to move; leaving the armchair, he begins to pace.

ANDERSON: I mean, I come to this city – to these buildings
here, this weird library – that oughtn't to be here any

more – and suddenly, out of nowhere, bang! I have a
whole new history . . .

MARILYN: And do you like your new history?

ANDERSON *pacing, with tea.*

ANDERSON: Yes! I think so . . .

I'm beginning to really wonder you know . . .

Because suddenly there's this dark romantic story –
(*He grins.*) Maybe even murderous! – and . . . (*He turns
to* MARILYN.) And on the surface – you know, I've
always been quite straight –

MARILYN (*smiles*): On the surface?

ANDERSON: On the surface yes – underneath I've always
felt, I've *always* known – there was another side.

You know that's why I came to a foreign city, to do
this great venture – get away from one's immediate
culture – be freer . . .

MARILYN: For your 'spontaneous business school'?

ANDERSON (*sharp grin*): Don't mock!

*He looks down at the pictures of Hettie that are spread
everywhere.*

ANDERSON: But it is – as the kids would say – an awesome
feeling . . . *Awesome* – to know this is part of me . . . part
of my blood! I mean everything I knew about my mother
. . . everything I thought about that side of my family –
it's all totally different . . . (*He smiles.*) Massively so . . .

He stops pacing. He looks at MARILYN.

ANDERSON: All sorts of things will change – I'll probably
dream differently . . . at night . . . (*He grins.*) All these
new dangerous images coming at me . . . !

MARILYN (*quietly watching him*): And that's exciting, isn't
it?

ANDERSON: You bet. It's amazing that you dug away – you
wanted there to be a story in my background – and there
was one!

MARILYN: There's probably something dangerous in all our

131

pasts . . . What was great about your grandmother – she loved being photographed.

ANDERSON: And I'm thinking – Oswald – It's really astonishing what he did. I mean just from my mother's picture!

His memory – he must have stored Hettie's face away in his memory – and somehow –

MARILYN: Yes he made the connection. He *did* have the Irish town as a clue –

ANDERSON: I wonder how quickly that happened –

We see the collection in strong evening light. OSWALD *is sitting at the table, in hard hat, with photos spread around him.*

ANDERSON (*voice-over*): He must have sneaked back here – after he came to see me – and started that little fire – he was in here, in his hard hat, doing his detective work . . .

We cut back to ANDERSON.

ANDERSON: No, he gave me that hat back, so it wasn't quite like that –

We see OSWALD *again, this time without the hat, exploring the photos.*

We cut back to ANDERSON.

ANDERSON: It was a feat of detective and memory work . . . I mean . . . it's uncanny.

MARILYN (*moving to phone*): It's not uncanny.

He has his own way of keeping records, it's not *all* memory, he has his own filing system . . . (*She smiles.*) It's just a bit different to most people's . . .

MARILYN *picks up phone.*

MARILYN: I'm going to call the hospital. I've got to see if there's been any change. (*As she dials.*) Buy the collection . . .

ANDERSON: What?

MARILYN: *Buy the collection.* You know very well if it had been split up – you would never have got the story about

132

your family.

She stares at him.

MARILYN: Buy it. . . .

The hospital answers.

MARILYN: Hello – can I have B wing please, the Aston
Ward?

*Her fingers are drumming nervously, we see how anxious she
is, about what news she might hear. She gets through to the
ward.*

MARILYN: Hello . . . I'm looking for information about Mr
Oswald Bates.

NURSE'S VOICE: What was that name again?

MARILYN: Mr Oswald Bates –

NURSE'S VOICE (*her voice serious*): Oh yes – please just hold
on for a moment.

MARILYN (*suddenly*): Oh shit . . . (*Her voice really loud.*) Oh
Christ . . .

She looks up, suddenly really upset.

MARILYN: I just heard her say something – you know – she
said something to another nurse 'About the gentleman
that just died' . . . I heard her say it . . . (*Holding phone
away from her very upset tears welling up.*) Oh, I can't
bear that, if that's true . . .

ANDERSON *is moving over to her.*

ANDERSON (*gently*): Just wait – overhearing like that – it
could be anybody . . .

MARILYN: I heard it . . .

NURSE'S VOICE: Just going to put you through to the
doctor now.

MARILYN (*into phone*): Has something happened? Could
you just tell me –

NURSE'S VOICE (*ignoring this, voice matter-of-fact*): I'm just
putting you through to the doctor . . .

Pause. MARILYN *looks up at* ANDERSON.

NURSE'S VOICE: He won't be a moment . . . can you hold?

MARILYN: Yes! You couldn't just tell me – (*She looks up furious.*) She's gone! – I don't think I can hold like this – why don't they just *tell* you? Get it done with?!

ANDERSON *takes the phone gently.*

ANDERSON: Shall I? . . . I'll hold.

MARILYN *moves across the room, then immediately turns.*

MARILYN: Has he come yet . . . ? Have they. come?

ANDERSON (*into phone*): Hello, no, OK . . . right . . .
(*He looks up at* MARILYN.) They're just coming . . .

MARILYN *is half praying.*

MARILYN: Please . . . Please . . .
If I believed . . . – this would be a time to pray!
(*With real force.*) Why am I not there?!

ANDERSON *watching her move backwards and forwards.*

ANDERSON (*simply*): You're great.

MARILYN: I'm great, am I . . . ?

ANDERSON: Yes – Marilyn . . . A great passionate person . . .

MARILYN: Passionate . . . ? I am, yes . . .

ANDERSON (*smiles*): And a wonderful storyteller.

MARILYN: Well . . . . Oswald's made me a great storyteller this week . . . He found it, I put it into words . . .

ANDERSON *watching her.*

ANDERSON (*then into phone*): OK . . . Right . . . . No, I'm a friend of Ms Truman's, yes . . . we're working together . . . I can take the message . . . yes . . .

He looks up and does a thumbs-up sign.

MARILYN *moves closer.*

ANDERSON: There's been a little improvement . . .

MARILYN *begins to cry . . . with shock, relief.*

ANDERSON *holds her, comforting her.*

INT. HOSPITAL. DAY.

OSWALD *is lying in a hospital bed. His eyes flickering slightly, not the deep coma.*

ANDERSON *and* MARILYN *stare down at him.*

ANDERSON: Well, I think . . . (*Then he stops.*) No, I won't
    say it . . .

MARILYN: What? (*She smiles.*) You were going to say – it's
    the only time you've seen him not talking!
    She bends down, her face close to OSWALD.

MARILYN: I want you to know we've followed Hettie's trail
    . . . and we found everything.
    OSWALD*'s eyes flicker.*

MARILYN: At least I *think* we've found everything . . .
    Slight noise out of OSWALD.

MARILYN (*smiles, but it suddenly flashes out of her*): And it
    was a deliberate test, wasn't it?! OF ME. Something I
    could have bloody well done without!

INT. A ROOM. ANOTHER COLLECTION. DAY.
We cut to MARILYN *sitting next to a table, looking straight
at us.*

MARILYN: So – did I win?
    Well, a little bit . . .
    *The camera moves through the collection, and then we cut
    back to* MARILYN.

MARILYN: Mr Anderson – for some reason I hardly ever
    called him Christopher – (*She smiles.*) Christopher
    Anderson got an American collection to buy the whole
    library – they got it cheap, and they didn't want it all –
    but we persuaded them.
    We see ANDERSON *looking more relaxed, different. A more
    emotional freer human being. He is moving past a wall of
    photos. We cut back to* MARILYN.

MARILYN: We *both* managed it. (*Broad smile.*) So it's still

ALL TOGETHER. For some other Oswalds to make startling connections between things . . . reveal other pieces of history . . . It's saved – but not in this country of course . . .

We see some of the most beautiful photos yet. Sumptuous images coming towards us, filling the screen. Then we suddenly see snaps of OSWALD *and* MARILYN *in a little wintry park, colour snaps of them walking together.*

We cut back to MARILYN.

MARILYN: And I'm bumbling along – working for another picture library . . . but soon I will try to get my own collection again . . .

We cut back to the snaps.

MARILYN: And Oswald is very gradually coming back to us . . . He'll never be the same. He has slowed right down, of course . . . I see a lot of him . . .

EXT. PARK. DAY.

MARILYN (*voice-over*): Often we go for walks and have slightly laboured conversations.

We see them moving in the park.

MARILYN: How much is genuine, how much he uses his new slowness for his own ends, I'm still finding out – OSWALD *and* MARILYN *sit side by side on a stone seat set in a wall in the park.*

MARILYN: Oswald . . . is this nearly right?

OSWALD *not looking at her – he is staring out across the winter park.*

MARILYN: You did what you did – your suicide attempt – because you saw all this change coming . . . like everybody's working lives are changing so completely . . . ? And your mind works really fast, you calculated *that's it* for me, probably won't get used again ever . . .

my career over – And you thought, better just check out
now – why waste time . . . ?

OSWALD *is eating crisps. He speaks very slowly,*
MARILYN *has to wait for each word.*

OSWALD: We're all hit by changing . . . things . . . can't . . .

MARILYN: Can't?

OSWALD: Not able to stop it . . .

MARILYN (*laughs*): It's like waiting for the Oracle to speak!
(*Giving him a warm shove.*) I have to listen to you even
more now – because it takes you so bloody long!

We cut back to MARILYN *staring straight at us, from
beside the table.*

MARILYN: He changed my life – I'm a lot more confident
dealing with the outside world now . . . And he changed
Mr Anderson's . . . In doing so he harmed himself . . .

I tell him many times that without the Oswalds of this
world – we have no future. None of us. They can do
things other people can't . . . And he likes hearing that
. . . (*She smiles.*) Naturally! . . .

We cut back to MARILYN *and* OSWALD *sitting next to
each other in the wintry park.*

OSWALD *is eating crisps. He stops.*

We move in on his face. He stares out at us. We hold on
OSWALD*'s face.*

Credits.

THE SHORTS

SPIG'S SHORT

SPIG *is sitting looking straight at us. She is in the upper gallery of the main hall of the collection, surrounded by books. She is sitting in a high-backed chair, confident and poised.*

SPIG: So – out of ten million photos we have here, which one have I chosen? (*She stares at us for a second.*) It wasn't difficult. I didn't have to think long, I picked the best picture I've ever seen on *fame*.
We see a picture of a man standing, full length, in the shadows of a large room which could be a studio or a large civic hall. We can just see a big expanse of wall, and this figure turned away from us, his hands raised up against the wall, as if he is about to be frisked. His head turned very slightly, half in shadow, half in light, but we cannot, tantalisingly, make out his features.

We cut back to SPIG.

SPIG (*grins*): Doesn't seem much I know, does it?! (*Then her face more serious.*) This picture was taken by the Danish photographer Holger Larsen, and he called it 'A Figure Apart'.
We see the picture again, this time just a little closer.

SPIG: A real 'so what' title I know . . .

So what's the big deal . . . ? (*She smiles conspiratorially.*) Holger Larsen produced this picture from his collection just before he died at the age of ninety-one, in 1988. He refused to say when he'd taken it, or where, but he did say there was one very interesting thing about it – he claimed that since he had taken the picture, the person in it –
We move closer towards the figure.

SPIG: This character here – had become one of the most *famous people in the twentieth century . . .* !

Close-up of SPIG.

SPIG: So – the great question is . . . WHO IS HE? Who is
this guy?!

We see the picture a little bit closer.

SPIG: Or is it just a hoax . . . ? A real tease by an old man on
his audience?

*We go in close on the clothes that look vaguely late forties or
early fifties but are not that specific.*

SPIG: Are the clothes the right period . . . ? Are the shoes
real . . . ? Or is the subject and the photographer
deliberately misleading us . . . ? It looks old but maybe
it's not that old.

We move in close on the half-turned face.

SPIG: And is it really a man? He is quite short . . . Could be a
woman – just.

We cut back to SPIG.

SPIG: I don't think it's a hoax . . . I think it's somebody who
was sure of his destiny, who collaborated with the
photographer to catch the very moment just before he –
or she – was about to become world famous . . .

We move around the picture again, SPIG*'s voice-over
leading back to her close-up.*

SPIG: We have a whole load of pictures here of people you
would know, people that became household names – we
have them *before* they became famous.

*We see pictures of Margaret Thatcher sitting at the knees of
somebody in a room at Oxford. We see film stars caught
looking ungainly, tentative . . . We see world leaders looking
sheepish and deferential . . . Obedient servants to their elders.*

SPIG: I love these pictures . . . ! Did they all know they were
destined for something big?

We see more faces.

SPIG: Did they really feel – they were on a path that could
only lead to one place? *Some* did I'm sure! . . . I'm
convinced of it!

We look into the eyes of the subjects.

SPIG: They didn't know how, and they didn't know when, but they KNEW something big was coming. Always felt it would happen . . .

Back to SPIG. *She is laughing.*

SPIG: But it's great, isn't it, seeing them down among the rest of us?!

And they really hate these pictures! They'd like to keep them away from the public for ever – they want us to think they plopped fully formed in front of us . . . Having already worked it all out. (*She grins.*) I wonder if they know that *I* know where there are pictures of them they'd really kill to stop being seen.

We see Clinton, Tony Blair, etc., when they were really young and awkward.

SPIG: Come to the collection and for a big enough fee I'll show them to you.

Back to the mysterious figure.

SPIG: So the question you are wondering is – do I know who this mystery character is? She better bloody tell us, you're thinking . . . (*She smiles.*) Ever since I've been working here, I've been figuring it out.

We move closer on SPIG.

SPIG: Sometimes I make it turn round for me . . .

We see a second picture of the figure turned towards us in a wide shot, we can't quite make out the face. We go back to SPIG *for a quick cut.*

SPIG: I imagine it moves and I see the face. And there is . . .

We go back to the figure, and the young face of Hitler is staring out at us.

SPIG: Maybe on another day, the figure turns . . . And it's Prince Charles!

We see Prince Charles's head on the figure.

SPIG (*grins broadly*): Wouldn't that be amazing, show a completely different side to him, wouldn't it?

143

We cut back to the picture and go through a series of quick cuts between SPIG*'s face and the picture, each cut has a different head on it.*

SPIG: Or Saddam Hussein . . . Or just an actress playing around . . . Julia Roberts or Audrey Hepburn . . . Or of course Elvis Presley – most people guess it's him – but I can tell you it's *not* Presley.

We go back to SPIG.

SPIG: And of course, sometimes when I'm alone I see the picture and the figure turns –

We see the photograph.

SPIG: *And it's me in the picture!*

We see SPIG*'s head on the picture.*

SPIG: And why not? I'm seeing the future! . . . Maybe . . . I can be happy working here – and also dream of being world famous. Nothing wrong in wanting both!

We cut back to SPIG.

SPIG: You will have guessed by now I don't know who the person is . . . BUT –

We go back to the picture, moving towards it from a distance. We keep moving closer, intercut with SPIG*'s face, until the picture is so close, it is abstract.*

SPIG: But I do know *something* . . . We have worked out it isn't *old*. The feel of the picture is modern, something about the lighting – this picture was taken some time in the sixties or seventies.

So maybe . . . Just maybe . . . The person who it really is will see this – will see themselves . . .

She stares into our eyes.

SPIG: And tell us.

She pauses for a moment. Then she smiles.

SPIG: But maybe they need to hurry up . . . because it could be their fame is already going. You don't want to wait too long . . .

Back to the picture, then back to SPIG.

SPIG: Because it would be terrible, wouldn't it – if they stepped forward and said 'It's me, it's me in the pictures! . . .'

And we said – 'And who are you? . . .'

Credits.

VERONICA'S SHORT

VERONICA *is sitting beside a table, staring at us in mid-shot.*
She is dressed in a smart but conservative dress, and is sitting
rather demurely, with a cup of tea next to her.

VERONICA: So these are the pictures I've chosen . . .

I think maybe you will think it is rather a surprising
choice.

We see pictures of Smithfield meat market during the war.

Porters moving meat, carcasses hanging up. People
passing by, going about their business, with the meat
hanging behind them.

VERONICA*'s voice continues, over the pictures.*

If you have ten million pictures – and we do have
some very beautiful ones, of course, amongst all that –
Why have I picked some pictures of meat?

We cut back to VERONICA, *sitting by the table.*

VERONICA: Well, it's certainly not because I'm a passionate
meat-eater, though like most people I enjoy a good roast.

We go back to the photographs, the street scenes, the meat
hanging up.

VERONICA: But it's because if you look carefully, and if you
know, then these pictures tell another story.

We see the smiling porters, with fags in their mouths and
their supervisors with small round glasses.

VERONICA: This is wartime . . . and of course food was
scarce – But something else is going on here, something
that I love to think about! And it is – I promise you –
absolutely, totally true.

We see meat being packed up. The camera getting closer and
closer to the pictures, moving away from the meat, on to the
packs of ice.

VERONICA: The *ice* is the clue . . .

We see the large blocks of ice.

VERONICA: In fact, these people –

We move in closely on the people, as they are caught in the photographs lifting the great blocks of ice.

VERONICA: These people are working for Winston Churchill on one of the most secret missions of the war.

We move among the meat porters of Smithfield.

> *As* VERONICA *tells us, we see the same images again of the busy meat market, now cast in a totally different light.*

VERONICA: Winston Churchill had the idea – because there weren't enough aircraft carriers . . .

Close-up of VERONICA *staring straight up into our eyes.*

VERONICA: And I swear this is true –

We go back to the ice and meat and the porters.

VERONICA: He had the idea to build ships out of ice, and to float the ice ships in the Atlantic, and to land our planes on them! They would have gritted their tops, I'm sure . . . the tops of the ships!

The camera slides across the pictures to find the old buildings that overlook the market.

VERONICA (*voice-over*): Behind these windows here, using the ice from the market, they are assembling a prototype – a great scale model . . . an ice aircraft carrier.

The camera moves closer and closer towards the window. It then cuts back to the porters and passers-by in the market.

VERONICA: And in fact these pictures, full of happy meat porters and butchers . . . are in fact crawling with agents, boffins and government officials . . . maybe a German spy . . . !

We see the faces of the market. Then we go back to the window.

VERONICA: And now . . . if we go close to the windows . . . right up to them . . .

We pass right up to the windows getting tighter and tighter so the picture becomes grainy.

VERONICA: You can just see the shape of the beautiful ice ship.

We move right up to the darkness, the grain filling the screen, and just a hint of the ghostly shape of a ship. Then the dots fill the screen.

VERONICA: That's the closest you'll get to seeing it –

You have to have worked with pictures a long time to know their secrets. There are a lot of stories in them.

We move among the magnified dots, getting deeper and deeper into the picture.

Credits.